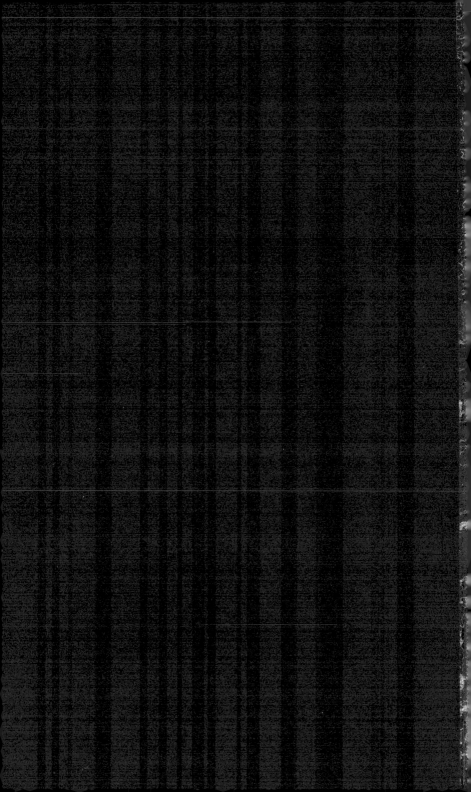

BOOK

ALSO BY WHOOPI GOLDBERG

ALICE

WHOOPI GOLDBERG

BOOK

Little, Brown and Company

A *Little, Brown* Book

Published by Little, Brown and Company (UK) 1998

First published in the United States by Rob Weisbach Books, an imprint of William Morrow and Company, Inc., New York 1997

A CIP catalogue record for this book is available from the British Library

ISBN 0 316 64570 2

Printed and bound in Great Britain by Clays Ltd, St Ives plc

Little, Brown and Company (UK)
Brettenham House
Lancaster Place
London WC2E 7EN

To Frank; my daughter, Alex;

my brother, Clyde; and my mom, Emma . . .

the soup from which this all flows

A grateful nod to Tommy, assistant extraordinaire; Dan Strone, agent extraordinaire; and Rob Weisbach, editor extraordinaire, who kept saying, "Would'ya? Could'ya? Don'tcha?" Well, I would, I could, I do . . .

and I did. Thanks.

RIFFS

It's not what you call me, but what I answer to.

—African proverb

FATE

AT BIRTH, I knew something was coming. As soon as I popped into the birth room, I looked over in a corner, and there was my old man Destiny smilin' at me.

My mother knew too. She felt I was gonna be special. Different. From the very beginning, she knew. The story she tells was that I came out—headfirst, of course—pulled one arm through, looked around the delivery room, turned to the light, put my thumb in my mouth, and stared right back at all the folks who were staring at me. The spotlight was on me for the very first time, and I guess I thought it was kinda cool. Hey, what's not to like?

I supposedly stayed that way for a while, in my serious, don't-mess-with-me pose; and from the way everyone was fussing, you'd think I'd taken a bow, or told a joke or something. The nurses and doctors started bringing in all the other nurses and doctors for a look. They'd never seen a kid make such an entrance, with such an attitude. They were coming in from all over, just to see.

Right then, I knew my life was gonna be different. Now I don't mean to leave the impression that I knew *exactly* what was ahead, 'cause it wasn't that way at all. I mean, I was a baby, right? A newborn. But I carried that moment with me to where I just figured I'd get a job, make some money, maybe leave my mark before I was through. I popped out knowing everything'd be fine.

And then some startling shit happened. I started thinking.

WIND

WE ALL FART, right? We all get that cramp that tells us there's an air bubble percolating in our butt and it needs to escape. But we don't like to talk about it. Everybody does it, and no one talks about it. Why is that?

Let's break this down. Let's consider the fart in all its wonder. The public fart is a very tricky thing. It's all tied up in where you are, and who you are, and who you're with, and what you ate for lunch. Most people, when they feel a fart coming on, they get up and make for the door, because they're not always sure what that little cramp is telling them. It could be a fart, or it could be one of those power dumps disguised as a fart. Have you ever had one of those? You go to let the air out a little bit and you're surprised by the actual materials you've deposited in your pants. Public farts are troubling enough, but these surprise power dumps are especially upsetting.

For the most part, a fart is a fart. We feel it coming. We know what it is. And we usually have enough butt control to drop 'em at will, or hold 'em back for a more appropriate time, or ease 'em out slow and silent. The game is in figuring out which approach to take, and then what to do with yourself after you've made your deposit.

I'm a great believer in claiming farts. Always have, always will. I don't want to be blamed for one of yours. Mine I know. Mine I can control. Yours, who the fuck knows what's going on down there?

I think there should be some sort of code word, some way to politely signal that you've got some business going on. It's common courtesy. I always call my farts tree monkeys, 'cause tree monkeys make the same farty sound as I do. It's a funny little sound. It would almost be cute, if it wasn't followed by the smell. It's like lightning and thunder. You get that funny little sound, and then the smell hits you. Sometimes it takes a few beats; sometimes it hits you right away. I just say, "Tree monkey," then I get up and walk away. I don't wait for it to hit. I go to the other end of the room and let people figure it out for themselves.

I love folks who say, "No, no, mine don't smell. I just farted, but it doesn't have any odor." Maybe to you, pinhead, but it stinks like shit to me. Some people actually enjoy the smell of their own farts, and that's fine if they do their farting at home, but when they take 'em out on tour they need to know. Mine, of course, are the exception to this rule. Mine aren't too bad, and this is not just my opinion. I've had corroboration on the violet scent of my behind. I should probably bottle it, and call it *Whoopi*. *Essence of Whoopi,* from Prince Matchabelli, you know.

Elevators are a problem. There should be some scanning device built into all new elevators that lets people know if there's a fart on board. Old elevators should be retired to accommodate the new ones. This would just be another common courtesy. Maybe there could be a big sign (FART ENCLOSED!) to warn people away. You have to know what you're dealing with before you step inside, because being trapped in an elevator with someone else's fart is one of the worst fates known to modern man. There's nothing you can do about it, and people have a right to know what to expect. The odor is bad enough, but there's also the responsibility. Somebody else always gets on the elevator and thinks it's yours, and you want to say, "No, no, no. This was here when I arrived. I have nothing to do with what this elevator cab smells like." But you can't say anything. If you say anything, they'll *know* it was you, or maybe they'll just *think* it was you, which pretty much amounts to the same thing. We're all so tense about our farts, and accounting for our farts. We can't even hold up a little yellow piece of notepaper that says, "This is not mine. This belongs to somebody else."

My mother had a great expression, "More room out than in," which basically meant, you know, that there's more room outside your body for this little air bubble than there is inside. More room out than in. It was a sweet little phrase, and it reminded me that farting is a natural thing. Holding on to it is unnatural, and it can lead to all sorts of problems. Ulcers. Gastrointestinal problems. A lot of those plumbing complications that hit us when we get older are caused or aggravated by holding on to your farts, so you've got to let fly.

I've had serious ulcers for years and years, and I'm now the fart queen, the ruler of all I pollute. If I'm not dropping air biscuits, something's wrong. A lot of people don't know this about me, and until now I've been refined enough to keep it to myself, but that's how I got my name, from my frequent farting. When I was in my twenties and diagnosed with ulcers, I was encouraged to fart up a storm, and my friends started calling me Whoopi. I was like a walking whoopee cushion, they said. It was an easy tag, and the name stuck. The name lingers, like a good fart, long after my violet scent has dissipated.

So it's a very healthy thing to do, and it's an unavoidable thing to do, and we should all just ease up a bit about it. There should be some basic rules, but we shouldn't go holding back and making ourselves sick. Yeah, there's more room out than in, but sometimes the outside environment is just not ready for you. People shouldn't be allowed to fart if they're standing on a crowded bus or subway, because their butt's in someone's face and it's just too lethal; it's a direct hit, and there's nowhere for the victim to turn. You shouldn't be allowed to fart on an airplane, because you can't exactly crack a window for relief. (Maybe, on international flights, they should set aside a few rows for farting.) And you shouldn't be allowed to drop one of those silent killers and not claim it, because those SBDs can indeed be deadly. Some farts should just have people's names on them, you know.

People have all kinds of techniques to avoid being found out. Some people keep pets around, so they can blame their farts on the cat. (Honey, cat farts bleach wood, they're so powerful.) Some genteel folks lift up one butt cheek, like a dog lifting his leg to pee, to allow the released air a clean path, but I don't understand this move. Do they think the fart won't find their clothes if they're not sitting down? Do they think it won't snake its way into the upholstery? They must think they're liberating the fart and sparing all the fabric in the room.

Some shy folks just hang in there quietly, not saying anything at all, hoping no one will notice, but these people are always an easy mark. When some wicked cheese hits you full in the face, they're the ones with the blank looks, like they don't know what's going on. How can they not know what's going on? It's obvious. *Whoever smelt it, dealt it*. That was a line from my childhood, but it was bullshit. Whoever *didn't* smell it was usually the dealer.

Fart strategy can be tricky. If you're at a party, or a meeting, and you have to drop a little biscuit, do you drop and sit or do you drop and cross the room? Does the smell go with you, or does it stay behind? To the best of my figuring, you're nailed either way, so it's probably better to stay where you are and let the seat cushions absorb the brunt of it. If you move around, you take it with you, and it's like leaving another fart on the other side of the room. There's no sense compounding the problem with a secondhand fart. If you're too chickenshit to cop to it, don't get up. Wait it out. And remember, just because you're sittin' on it doesn't mean it's not gonna snake its way up and around you. It's gas, and it will come up through your thighs, and people are gonna know it's you anyway. But if you just keep on talking, then suddenly stop and look around to see where that mystery smell came from, that could add to the effect.

• • •

The stage gives a great perspective on farts and farting. You look out across those lights, and you can just see the farts on people's faces. The smells don't always find you, all the way up on the stage, but those facial expressions make it plain. In a Broadway house, a lot of the people hurry through a pretheater dinner to make the curtain, and they all bring their farts with them. You'll see someone's eyes pop out, really big, like in one of Rodney Dangerfield's double takes. Or you'll see people squirming in their seats, all crinkled up, like they're trying to hold something back. And then you'll see the people looking around in desperation. They've got their noses pointed up, scoping out some clean air. And you can almost see the gas float from one row to the next, like in a Pepe Le Pew cartoon. The people just fall like dominoes. I always look for the person who's sitting up straight, pretending he doesn't smell anything. He's almost always the culprit, because the key to dropping a fart is you have to smell it too. You have to look as indignant as everyone else. You can't protest too much, in case they trace it back to you, but you've got to protest a little. You've got to go through the motions.

Among the cast and crew, there's a whole farting convention. When I was in *Forum,* on Broadway, there were several noted farters onstage, and there was all kinds of running around in the show, so a lot of times the fartee discovered the fart before the farter was even aware of it. When you're moving around like that, you don't always know. You leave a little trail. Stuff happens. You leave it so people run through your farts when they're crossing the stage. It's like hitting a wall, and they're breathing hard so they've already inhaled it. It's in their lungs.

After a while, you start to recognize each other by the smells you leave behind. Oh, that's Corey. And that one there, that's Whoopi. You just look over at someone and think, That's from your ass, I can tell. You also start to recognize what people have been eating, because certain foods make you fart in certain ways. Beans don't get me the way they get other people. Processed meat always does me in. Deli sandwiches are my fiercest enemy when I'm doing a show, 'cause that luncheon meat makes me very chatty. Chocolate too. I tend to stay away from chocolate if I'm gonna be out and about. And it's not just food that determines the tone and tenor of my anal conversation. When I'm on antibiotics, I can empty a building. Very few medications agree with me, but antibiotics yield the most stunning brew. I'm surprised I've never been arrested, or committed, for some of the smells that have come out of me when I'm taking medicine.

Relationship farts are a whole other deal. The goal here is to contain yourself until you've gotten past the I-don't-want-to-take-a-dump-in-your-bathroom-because-I-don't-want-you-to-know-my-shit-stinks phase. Once you can stink up his toilet, you can let fly with impunity, and you want to get to this place fairly soon in a relationship because you don't want to misrepresent yourself to the other person. Love me, love my farts. Love me, and know that periodically you're gonna open the bathroom door and get killed.

I resent under-the-cover farts. They're just not fair. I'm not talking about sex farts. I've never experienced those, at least not during the act itself. After you've done the deed, you're up and you're loose and sometimes you let one go, and when that happens it's kinda funny. It's animalistic, but it's playful and it's okay. During the night, though, when I'm sleeping, it's just not fair. It's also animalistic, but it seems to involve only *dead* animals. I'm sorry, but some of those sleep farts wake you in the middle of the night and you think to yourself, What crawled up his ass and died? It's a powerful visual, but really the best way to describe how some of these things can smell.

Ultimately, little kids have got the best handle on this farting business. They've got all kinds of great names and games for it. They pull each other's finger. They light each other's farts. They fart out the alphabet, on cue, or they belt out a cute marching tune. They're proud of their farts and what they can do with them. The louder and wetter and smellier the better. I sometimes try to imagine what the world would be like if we were more like kids in this way. God knows, our elevator rides would never be the same. The cars would be so thick with fart gas we couldn't see our way to the buttons. At work, we'd punctuate our presentations at both ends. We'd fart in each other's faces, and laugh and laugh, and it would be a good thing to give off such a foul smell that it turns someone's skin a different color. Guys with the best farting skills would get all the babes, and we'd be farting up a storm and feeling good about ourselves all over again, for no reason at all.

TRUST

I DON'T CARE how many people our presidents have slept with. I truly don't. It doesn't take away from who they are or what they're about or what they might accomplish. Just because a guy gets his tip wet once in a while, it doesn't make him a bad president. It doesn't even make him a bad guy. It's just part of the human package.

Take John Kennedy—this young, good-looking guy who believed that everyone was created equal and that you could do things within your reach, within your sphere, and make the world a better place. This notion, that we could all make a difference, flowed from JFK into our schools and our neighborhoods. It didn't matter that he was fucking Marilyn Monroe. It mattered that he got us thinking in this civic-minded way. What mattered was that he had us believing we mattered. It's a dusty sentiment from a long time ago, but for me it came from folks like Kennedy and Martin Luther King and Medgar Evers, and it has stayed with me, no matter what shit journalists and historians have been digging up on any of these guys. The scandals might be titillating, but they're just not relevant.

It's the same today. Take any politician from my generation and ask them how many people they've slept with, or what kinds of drugs they've ingested, or where they stood on Vietnam, and you know you're bound to piss off someone with the answer. The people who smoked dope, the people who didn't . . . You can't be all things to all people, and you're fucked if you try.

Look, for all we know, the prez is a great husband. We don't know what goes on in a marriage, but we do know that being married doesn't mean you will never fuck up. We all fuck up. Presidents just fuck up on a public stage. Has this president made some mistakes in his marriage? Maybe. But what president hasn't? Eisenhower? Roosevelt? A lot of these cats we now think of as great presidents were getting a little something on the side, but it didn't make them any less presidential. It just came with the territory.

Did Bill Clinton, as governor, come on to Paula Jones? We'll never know for sure, but we can think it through. This man was the governor of Arkansas. Come on, it would have been pretty stupid if he did. But, okay, even smart people do stupid things. Maybe he did make a play for her, and she wasn't into it. Maybe she was into it and then pulled back. Or maybe it didn't happen at all. Who knows? I just can't imagine that he took his penis out and waved it at her. *That's* something you'd holler about right away. You know, if you're concerned about the man's ethics and the moral fiber of this country, then you go out right away and say, "The governor of this state just pulled his penis out and waved it at me and I want to stop him from ever doing it again." That's the time to do it.

I felt the same way about Anita Hill and Clarence Thomas. If things went down like Anita Hill said they went down, then why leave the asshole on the job to keep harassing other women? File the complaint. You don't wait five years and expect to be taken seriously. I'm sorry, you just don't.

But that shit doesn't matter, because ultimately what happened, or didn't, is between Bill Clinton and Paula Jones. The president will have to deal with his own mess, and it's none of our fucking business. I don't care if he boned a sheep, if that's his thing. Some people like sheep. I've never tried one, so I can't say whether or not this is a good thing, but where a president puts his penis has nothing to do with the work he did in Arkansas or New York or Kennebunkport or Boston, or what he can still do in Washington. I can't look at this man and say, "You, because you came on to this woman and showed her your weenie, you are not equipped to make decisions on my behalf." That's crap. Shit like this happens every day. Decisions are being made by passionate people doing things in their personal lives that I would not do in mine. Are they bad guys? I don't think so. Maybe they're just misguided, or misinformed, or horny.

Look, men in power get laid. They do. And when pussy calls there are a lot of men who respond. Men do that. Sadly, the inverse hardly ever happens, at least not to me. Power makes women masculine in the eyes of most men. This is what I've been told. That's why people get so pissed off at Hillary Clinton. They think, Well, you know, she just wants to be him. I think, No, she knows what the fuck she's doing, she's all right. But people don't want to hear it because power and sexuality in women does not compute. Men don't throw themselves at you. They want to take the lead. That's the way they've been brought up, and women have been brought up to play into that. I'm sorry, but we have. It's why Marcia Clark can bust her butt, on a public servant's salary, and still be second-guessed because she had to put her kids in day care in order to go to work. Guys don't have to put up with that shit; they're expected to work their butts off. But when a woman does it, she has to apologize for neglecting her children.

There's a huge double standard. It's not just about sex, it's about everything, and when it starts to fuck up our politics it gets me pissed off. We've allowed our two-party system to become about cutting the other guy off at the knees, and the easiest way to do that is to dig up some dirt on your opponent. This is what passes for debate in a modern democracy: "Yeah, maybe I have cheated on my wife, but you have a thing for transsexuals." This is what we've become, and in a relatively short space of time.

Until Watergate, we never really paid much attention to what went on behind closed doors in Washington. Office doors, bedroom doors, we just didn't want to know. But then, suddenly, we looked Richard Nixon in the face and saw ourselves. It was a traumatic thing. Nixon was the full catastrophe, but he was real and tangible and human. And the people thought, This is just too much. So we started looking for leaders who were infallible, thinking we would someday hit on the right guy. Gerald Ford was a decent guy, with a great wife and shaky legs, but he was too ordinary. Jimmy Carter was wholesome and sincere and different, and he had his own good woman at his side, but then he went and "lusted in his heart" in a *Playboy* interview. (Who the hell lusts in his heart? Go out and lust in the haystack, or the peanut shed, or wherever a good old farm boy is meant to do his lusting. And don't go tellin' *Playboy* about it when you're through.)

For a while Ronald Reagan had us thinking he was the savior. Or maybe folks just had themselves convinced he'd ride in on his white horse and clean out the mess and fight back the bad guys and leave us all in peace and prosperity. No one asked if he was getting any extra nooky on the side, because no one cared.

By the time we reached George Bush and his thousand points of light, we didn't think to ask about *his* extramarital affairs. We ran Gary Hart out of town 'cause he turned up on a boat in Bimini with Donna Rice, but we seemed to hold George Bush to a different standard. Did we crucify Gary Hart because of his transgression, or because of the manner of his transgression? If it was the latter, man, we gave this guy a raw deal. Somebody took Gary Hart's picture on a boat and sold it to the tabloids. I understand how that happens. Does it mean he was boning this woman in the middle of a campaign? Maybe, maybe not. But with Bush, it was considered unseemly to even bring it up, and then this lady surfaced and started crowing about how she'd been sleeping with him for years, which in itself is kinda scary. But it didn't matter. We liked George enough to let this one slide, and we liked Barbara a whole lot more and were not about to dignify the allegations with our suspicions, because, you know, we didn't want to upset her any more than the situation already had.

With Clinton, the character debate wasn't only about his sex life. It was about Vietnam, and dope, and his ability to shift with the tides. It was about this young guy who didn't fight in his generation's war, or inhale his generation's dope. Forget that he thought Vietnam was an unjust war, as we can all now pretty much agree. Forget that. He didn't do like everyone else. He didn't do like his opponents. They were there. "We saved the world," they said, but they made it seem that Clinton's actions stood for something more than a generational difference in thinking. There was no discussion about the ethics of a whole generation—mine, and Clinton's—because our ethics weren't the ethics of George Bush and Bob Dole. The Republicans talked a lot about going to Vietnam and fighting for the "right thing," but to some of us it was a little vague what that right thing actually was.

I just kicked back and looked at the whole thing as a big old poop pile, and by now it's gotten to where we will never find another candidate from either party who's gonna come up smelling like a rose unless he's been in a box his entire life. And who wants a candidate who's been in a box his entire life? We've all done stuff we wish we hadn't, said things we wish we could just suck back in our faces and leave unsaid, taken positions that no longer reflect our views. Does that negate what we're doing now? No way.

Bill Clinton could be a great president. He knows what he's done, and he knows what he's doing. Judge him on what he does in office, as president. Should politicians be held to a higher standard of behavior than the rest of us? Absolutely, but we need to be realistic, and we need to recognize that if the behavior is okay with

Jackie and Barbara and Hillary and company, then we've got no cause to bitch.

Hey, Clinton copped to smoking that joint (although I could have done without the questionable inhaling crap, but maybe he'll cop to that one day too). He copped to Gennifer Flowers, and the Republicans may even find something for him to cop to in Whitewater or his campaign-financing mess. And we'll make him cop to every last piece of indecision or cowardice or bad judgment, and in the end what will count is whether or not we think this man has the stones and the heart and the mind to lead this country in a positive direction. Do we believe in what he stands for, and in what he's trying to accomplish? Or do we just want to slap another scarlet letter on yet another person just to help us to feel a little better about ourselves?

Decide, people. Decide.

HEAD

I LIVE WITH A WONDERFUL MAN. I've lived with other men in my life too, and not a single one of them has had a clue what he was doing in the bathroom. Not a clue. I don't care how wonderful or presumably wonderful a man is. Surround his ass with tile and porcelain and his head explodes.

I'll tell you what: It doesn't matter how big the damn sink is. A man can't shave or wash without splashing water all over the place. You'd think after all that time standing in front of the sink looking in the mirror, he'd have some idea where to find his face, but from the way he splashes, it's clear he's just hoping to hit his target once in a while. He'll settle for that. They throw the water all over their heads, but they're not shaving their heads. Why does there have to be water everywhere? And why can't they shave in the shower? Haven't they seen those shower mirrors in the hardware store? They're available, you know they're available, so just pick your ass up, go down to the store, and start shaving in the fucking shower.

To most men, this is a ridiculous proposition. They would sooner sing on the subway than shave in the shower. They don't see the need. They just splash all that water around and figure it'll dry up eventually, and it *will* dry up eventually, except that I'm gonna be using that bathroom long before eventually. I have to add five minutes to my routine just to blot down the mess. It gets to where I'm cleaning the bathroom every time I go in there. And then, when you start moving stuff around, you see it's all moldy underneath from all that water, and the little cleanup turns into a giant production. It starts to take all day just to go in and brush out your hair—not that I have much call to brush out my hair. And you can't talk to him about it, because you just can't. You bring it up and a fight begins:

"You're not letting me be myself."

"What do you mean, I'm not letting you be yourself? I'm living with you. I'm sharing a bathroom with you. What the fuck does the way you splash water around when you shave have to do with being yourself?"

"Well, you're coming in anyway. You're gonna use the sink anyway. It's just gonna get all wet again, so what's the point?"

"The point is, I don't want to wipe up your mess, day after day. You made the mess. Wipe it up!"

And it's not just water. If it was just water, maybe I could deal. But there's hair, and dried-up toothpaste spit, and gobs of mucus, and beard stubble, and little pee spots all over the seat and floor, and who knows what else? Who wants to come in and look at that? Who wants to touch it? It's enough of an ordeal to touch my own mess, but touching someone else's . . . Yeccchhh! Please!

Now, this shit doesn't happen at the beginning of a relationship, because that's the oh-baby-you're-so-wonderful period. That's when they get you. No one wants to be found out during the oh-baby period. Men chew their food before they talk, they don't leave their crusty underwear on the floor, they don't piss in the sink. Yes, men actually piss in the sink. Not right away, but they get to it. Apparently it's a great burden to them to walk those extra five feet to the toilet, so they go in the sink. At first, you have some idea this has been going on, because like I said, their aim is off, especially late at night. But then you catch them at it and call them on it.

"What the fuck are you doing? I have to use that sink. I soak my panty hose in that sink. I close the drain and fill it up with water and use it to wash my face. What's wrong with you? You don't pee in your mother's sink."

"Just rinse it out," he'll say.

Just rinse it out? Yeah, like that'll cover it. You know, come on. Just come on. Hand me the Lysol and stop peeing in the sink.

And when you've been together long enough, he'll just go in the sink right in front of you. There's no pretense. You'll be using the toilet and he just can't wait. He's got to go. He has to pee in the sink. There's got to be something to this, something primal. Maybe it's a marking-territory kind of thing, to keep the enemies at bay. Maybe it's a fraternity thing, because frat boys just have no sense of how to behave when it comes to their bodily functions; they could be eighty years old and still think it's a hoot to leave a lit bag of shit on someone's doorstep.

The pissing in the sink is bad enough, but there's other stuff. As the days go by, there are more spots around the tub, or on the floor. The shower isn't rinsed out, there are pubic hairs on the soap, the bathtub has a ridge of scum around it. This is the wake-up period when you realize you're deep into the same old shit. The oh-baby period is over and you've been had. You think to yourself, Where am I? Who is this person I moved in with? When will I learn?

I'm just as bad, I suppose. We women have got our own weird behaviors. Me, I have lotions. All over the place, I have lotions. Moisturizers, remoisturizers, post-moisturizers, every damn cream you can find, meant to do every damn thing to your skin. You make it, I'll buy it, and then I'll line it up in my bathroom and arrange it in sequence with all the others. Then I have my different soaps, because one day I'll want to smell like peppermint and one day I'll want to smell like almonds and one day I'll want to be all tutti-frutti. I'll have eight or nine going at the same time. And you can't have just one shampoo. You've got to have the shampoo that feeds the hair, the shampoo for when your scalp is dry, the shampoo that deals with split ends, the shampoo that adds luster. (Because, darling, you can never have too much luster.)

He'll look at all my creams and shit and wonder what I'm doing. I can see that, I guess. I can see how all my lotions and soaps and shampoos would freak a guy out, especially when I won't let him touch any of it or move the stuff around. I use them all in order. I start with this and then I do this and then I do this. The sequence is key. I don't want no guy coming in and messing with my sequence.

Finally, when we've each pretty much had it with the other person, one of us will suggest we have separate bathrooms. This is the desperation period, because most people can't afford separate bathrooms. It's not practical. Even if you can afford it, who's gonna be the one to have to walk down the hall to use the bathroom at the other end of the house? Who wants to pee in Siberia?

Most people probably don't want separate bathrooms, deep down. It runs counter to the notions of partnership and sharing and commitment behind most relationships. Once you're living together, separate bathrooms are one step away from separate bedrooms, or maybe those separate twin beds, like Rob and Laura Petrie used to have.

So the thing to do is get along. Or try. Figure out what kinds of things come out of and go into each other's bodies, or on each other's skin. Ladies, know that your man is gonna miss the toilet from time to time, or splash water around while he's shaving, or leave his pubic hairs on the soap. Learn to adjust. And that goes for you men too. Don't get all bent over a box of sanitary napkins. Once in a while, we're gonna leave them out for a few days, 'cause it's easier than ducking into that cupboard underneath the wet sink every time we need one. And we've got a whole assortment: different sizes for the underpants of the day, others for heavy days, and others for light days . . . we're just trying to cover all the bases.

And while we're on the subject, why is it that no man wants to hear about your period? They say, "Oh, you got your period?" Then they leave the room. Maybe they want us to go off in the woods for a few days and get it over with. They think we bleed like we've been shot, and they think we're gonna be all cranky.

Well, yeah, sometimes we get cranky. Just deal with it. Part of it is hormonal, but part of it is just being reminded that we have to deal with it ourselves. Every month we have to deal with it. And part of it is just tactical. The stuff they sell us to absorb the flow of menstrual blood doesn't always work the way it's supposed to. Sometimes, you bleed right through your clothes and people notice and move away from you and point you out to their children. Sometimes, with the glue they've got now at the bottom of these sanitary napkins, you can step the wrong way and glue yourself down. Let me tell you, there's nothing worse than walking down the street, doing your "Charlie" bounce, or your *That Girl* slide, swinging your bag, swinging your hair, and then one of your pubes gets caught in that sticky stuff. Your eyes well up, you can't move, you just turn cold and then hot. And it's not like we allow each other to scratch our butts in public. You can't stop to scratch or adjust yourself. You can't just turn to the guy next to you and smile sheepishly and say, "Oh, dear, my pubes are stuck." You've just got to reach in there and do what you have to do and hope no one you know is watching.

Tampons are a different bother. They're almost never moisturized, which means they've got to go in with kind of a push, and it hurts like hell, and as many men can tell you, it's probably no picnic for the tampon either; you need a little lubrication. And then you have to squat, or straddle the bowl if you're in a public rest room, and fiddle with the cardboard and the string and do the best you can, but the best you can still leaves you with a little string dangling from your vagina. I don't know about you, but I walk around feeling like one of those wooden marionettes. You know, pull my string and my arms'll flap up and down. It's just too fucking ridiculous.

And here's a classic argument. Women don't understand men not putting the seat back down, and men don't get what the big deal is. Guys come in, they lift up the toilet seat. Fine. This, in itself, is a good thing, because who wants to sit on it when they're through? But then, when they're done, why don't they put the seat back down? It's common courtesy. They know the next person to use the bowl will probably be someone else, unless they've got a bladder problem. They're probably thinking, She knows I'll be using the toilet after her, so why doesn't she just leave the seat up?

Well, the argument is in the math. Most people, for most business, sit down. I sit down all the time. He sits down some of the time. And the only people who poop standing up are little kids. So let's say that about 67 percent of the time the toilet will be receiving a sitting customer, which means that the toilet seat, in its ready position, should be down. End of story. Put the seat down.

I have touched cold water in the middle of the night more times than I care to remember. And not everybody flushes in the middle of the night, because they don't want to wake the other person. It's amazing to me that guys can be so selectively considerate, but this just compounds the problem. This just means, when you hit cold water, that you know what you've landed in. You're thinking, Oh, fuck, fuck, fuck. If you're like me, you have to get up and take a shower, because no way are you going to bed with a butt dipped in piss and who knows what else, but then the shower wakes him up and he starts yelling.

"Well, why the fuck are you taking a shower at three o'clock in the morning?"

"Because you didn't put the seat down, asshole."

And then you're off and running. You're mad. He's mad. You argue. You realize you're ill-suited. You break up. You end up on Skid Row. Why? All because of the goddamn toilet seat.

There's definitely too much going on in the bathroom for couples not to bump into each other and piss each other off. There's no getting around it, short of sending the guy out into the woods to do his business, which actually isn't a bad idea. Most men I know wouldn't mind. Let 'em pee against a tree, and sharpen a piece of slate against a rock and use it to shave, and take a dump out behind the bushes and wipe their asses with a leaf, and leave you to enjoy your nice, dry bathroom. But you want to keep him at least somewhat domesticated. Let him in once in a while. Run the shower on him. Brush his teeth with running water. Remind him how things are done, because you don't want to take him out to a dinner party and find him peeing in the punch bowl. Most people are particular about their punch bowls. They just are.

HOME

MY BROTHER, CLYDE, is a big old guy. He's six years older than I am, and when you're a kid, those six years are big. When I was growing up, if somebody was bothering me, I could always tell Clyde. He backed me up, and I adored him. I still do. When you open the dictionary to *cool,* Clyde's picture is there. Clyde has his own theme music. When he walks down the street or into a room, you can hear him coming.

We were partners, growing up. It was just me and my mother and Clyde, in our little apartment in Chelsea. We all looked out for each other. The whole neighborhood looked out for each other. There was a real mix on our street: White people. Black people. Spanish people. Chinese people. Italian people. Every kid spoke ten lines of every language. You needed to be able to ask if so-and-so was home. Can I use the bathroom? Yes, I'll stay for dinner. And you had to be able to say hello to your friends' mothers on the street, to show them the proper respect.

It was a real neighborhood, you know. We had our yard, in the middle of four or five buildings. There was a barrel, and monkey bars, and a hopscotch board, and a group of mothers sitting on a bench, watching. We were always being watched. If you were fucking up, somebody on the bench would catch you at it. Or they'd be looking out the window, from upstairs.

There was no escaping the eye of the neighborhood, and it was always incredible to me what these women picked up on. You knew the lady next door was gonna tell your mother if you had eight kids up in the apartment. You knew all these mothers were watching your ass. Hillary Clinton was right. It *does* takes a village, and in Chelsea, around Twenty-sixth Street and Tenth Avenue, there was a whole lot of villaging goin' on.

These women had some sort of maternal radar that tipped them to when you were just considering doing something. You knew if someone caught you making out in the building's stairwell, your mother would find out. In the stairwell, everybody knows your business, so my mother's thinking was, If you're gonna experiment, there's no reason to be groping in the stairwell and exposing yourself to ridicule and gossip and everything. Better you should be in the house, and if it gets further than you want it to get, you can stop it by opening a door. You couldn't always put a stop to things in a stairwell.

There was also a neighborhood ear. If something happened, you could yell up to an open window and a grown-up would be downstairs in no time. If you fell and broke your leg, an ambulance would arrive before it occurred to you to feel any pain. Everything was immediate, because people were paying attention. And everybody's parents felt some responsibility in keeping all us kids in line. If you messed up, some adult would swoop in out of nowhere and bust your ass.

When I was little, my mother was a nurse at French Hospital, which is now an apartment building, and later on she became one of the best Head Start teachers in the city. But on the weekends and most summer evenings, she took up her post, just like all the other mothers. I'd yell up to our window—"Ma! throw me a quarter!"—and she'd stick her head out. When the Mister Softee truck pulled up and we all called up, you could see the curtains fluttering. It's like the whole building shook. Every parent knew their kid's call. You could call from across the street, and they'd know. They'd stick their heads out the windows and holler back, "Don't yell! Just come upstairs!"

But you didn't want to come upstairs because you might miss something. Someone might open the fire hydrant, and start this wonderful fountain, and you didn't want to miss that just to run upstairs for a quarter. All they had to do was wrap it in a napkin and toss it out the window. The napkin was so you could find it in the bushes, after it landed. My mother always tried to drop the quarter into the bushes, because, you know, they always said you could kill someone if you dropped a quarter on them.

In Chelsea, in the early sixties, you were rich with a quarter. A quarter could get you an ice cream and a couple of penny pretzels, a Tootsie Roll, maybe a few Jelly Royals. You could get Mary Janes, if you liked them, but I never did. Or you could get four or five packages of Dots. Or Bonomo Turkish Taffy. Remember Bonomo Turkish Taffy? That's what I really miss. You put it in the refrigerator, to get it hard, and then you took it downstairs and smacked it against the sidewalk so it broke into a hundred pieces for your friends.

There was just too much going on to run upstairs. In the summertime, Joe Papp's Shakespeare in the Park would come through the neighborhood, and you'd see all kinds of wonderful people putting on all kinds of wonderful plays. They'd pull up in this truck and in an hour they had the bleachers set up, and a stage. The truck would be open and magic things would be coming out of it. An hour later, just as the sun was going down, it would be time for the play. It was like the circus coming to town, and on those nights our little neighborhood was the center of the fucking universe. The theater came to us. And it was free.

The rest of the year, movies were our big treat. My mother took us all the time. Or we watched the *Million Dollar Movie* together on television. Or the *Late Show,* or the *Late, Late Show.* John Garfield . . . Honey, that man made me crazy as a kid. Just something about him. Or Carole Lombard. Goddess! When I saw Carole Lombard coming down some stairs in a long satin thing, I thought, I can do that. I wanted to come down those stairs, and say those words, and live that life. I knew it was all fantasy, but it seemed like so much fun. You could go to a double feature and see the same actress in two completely different roles. You could be anything, up there in the movies. You could do anything. You could fly. You could meet alien life forms. You could be a queen. You could sleep in a great big bed, with satin sheets, in your own room.

Nothing could make me laugh like one of those Tarzan movies on Saturday morning. Remember Tarzan? Big ol' hunk, swinging in the jungle, scaring the natives? Who were all black. Ain't it funny that this white guy, who was raised by a monkey, could control all those black folks? Shit, Daryl Gates could've used his ass during the L.A. riots. Anyway, I loved how Tarzan and Jane were living in sin, but I never understood that relationship. And whose kid was Boy? The best I could figure was he was like Swee' Pea, in *Popeye.* He arrived in a plane wreck at just the time Tarzan and Jane were ready for a kid. They were no longer a pair of loose jungle lovers, but a respectable jungle couple.

I loved the cartoons too. Especially the cartoons. *Betty Boop. Coco the Clown.* The early *Popeyes* had shadows drawn into them. In *Ali Baba and the Forty Thieves,* there were shadows in the sand, and the background was moving, and the characters were moving. The animation was amazing. And all the great big-band music underneath. "Minnie the Moocher." "St. James Infirmary." Cab Calloway, for real, just melting into the cartoon. Man, it was heaven.

We didn't see black and white then, not in my neighborhood. Movies were movies. There weren't black movies or white movies. It was all one fantasy. We didn't see it in each other, either. We were just friends and neighbors, trying to get along. There were assholes, like in any neighborhood, but there weren't black assholes and white assholes. There were big assholes and little assholes.

The civil rights movement didn't really mean much to me as a kid. In New York, it didn't resonate the way it did in the rest of the country. It wasn't about being able to drink from the same fountain or ride the same bus, because we could already do pretty much everything. I could go anywhere. There was no place that was restricted to me. No museum. No store. I could go into Tiffany's if I wanted. That time, to me, was all tied up in Vietnam and the Black Panthers and the Young Lords and the riots at Columbia.

It wasn't until I was an adult that I learned from my mother that her business was more welcome in some stores than in others. She wasn't denied access anywhere, but few department stores would give her a credit card. The first store that ever gave her a credit card was Barneys, on Seventeenth Street, and that's where she dressed my brother, Clyde. She was a loyal customer, especially after she got her credit card, but I liked the jingle for Robert Hall. "When the prices go up, up, up, the value goes down, down, down." Barneys didn't have a jingle, but they gave my mother a credit card.

We took our little trips. The Circle Line. The Statue of Liberty. Walking up to the crown took forever, but looking down was like magic. Coney Island was the best, though. The Wild Mouse. The Cyclone. Nathan's. Two or three times every summer, my mother would pack a big old picnic and take us out to Brooklyn. She prepared a great feast: fried chicken, celery, ham and cheese sandwiches, Kool-Aid, Ring-Dings. A treat day, my dear! Then she'd pack it all in this giant plastic carrier. There were no coolers or Tupperware in those days, just a big old heavy container she gave to Clyde to carry, and he was big and strong enough to lug it along without minding.

Coming out of the subway tunnel in Manhattan and shooting into the hot, open light of Brooklyn was the most exciting thing. I never tired of it. I'd look around, and wonder who was living there, and what their lives were like. It was like alighting onto foreign territory. And then, finally, the doors would open at Coney Island and I'd be hit by that smell: caramel apples, popcorn, hot dogs, and urine. There's no mistaking that smell. It washed over me, and I was gone. The beach, salt water, fried dough, cotton candy.

I knew how the day would go. I'd get off the train and hit the booths they had laid out to gear you up for the midway downstairs. I'd step out into all those booths and want everything all at once. I was big into this Kewpie doll they used to sell. She was pink and purple and blue, with sprinkles and feathers, and she was all I wanted. The day would fly. I'd watch my mother on the rides, and try to spot Clyde on the parachute, way up in the sky. I'd get on the Wild Mouse and yell myself hoarse. We'd walk from one end of Coney Island to the other, and see the sky go from bright, bright to dusky dusk. And then we'd climb back on the hot subway, with me holding cocktail stirrers shaped like a skull and crossbones, with two rhinestone eyes, that my mom had won playing Skee Ball, or some stuffed animal Clyde had won for me on the midway.

But as cool as it was to head out for Coney Island, just the three of us, or to the Statue of Liberty, or the movies, it was even cooler coming home. To have *been* there was somehow sweeter than actually *being* there, you know. And to have been there and back, to come home and tell the other kids about the adventure, to reclaim our own little world, where everyone knew everyone else, where there was no such thing as rich or poor, where we belonged . . . well, this was the greatest thing of all.

SELF

THE HARDEST THING in the world is to get along with one other person, 'cause they're not you. It's basic. People will disappoint you all the time. Expect it. Realize that people are different and not everybody is gonna think like you. Some people will just knock you out with their ridiculousness, but that's them, you know. That's not you.

I sometimes think, in a perfect world, if everyone was me, I wouldn't have to work so hard to get my point across, to be understood, to be left alone. I wouldn't have to deal with any stubble in the bathroom sink, unless I was shaving my own damn legs. I wouldn't have to deal with someone treating me like shit, or disregarding what I know, or coming into the room acting like God, because, honey, when you're meeting me, you're meeting God. And there can't be two Gods. I wouldn't have to make my relationships work, because they would just be with another me. I already know me, I can deal with me, so there'd never be a problem.

Then again, it could get incredibly dull—a world filled with only me. There'd be no surprises. I'm smart, and funny, and outrageous, but only in relation to everyone else. Would I be interesting to myself, multiplied? I don't think so. I'd run out of things to say before too long. I'd have nothing to be pissed off about, and I couldn't piss anyone else off either. That's the key to our relationships anyway, isn't it, that we're all a little different? We don't look for someone just like us. We want to be pushed, challenged, taken in new directions. There are people out there who have ideas that are not yours that sort of stop you in your tracks and get you thinking in new ways. It's a healthy thing. It's a good thing. It's essential.

When it's just you, you never have to live up to your own expectations. What the hell for? It's just you, right? When it's just you, you never have to put yourself out there or take chances. When you think about it, as I for some reason have, you realize that it could never be just you, cloned, a million times over. It wouldn't be a world filled with Whoopi Goldbergs, all thinking the same things, all at the same time. There'd be a me in a clean mode, and another me in a sloppy mode, so there's already tension. There'd be a carefree me, and a pissy me; a liberal me and a conservative me; a rich me and a poor me. For every crossroads in my life, for every decision I've made, there'd be a Whoopi who went in this direction and a Whoopi who went in that direction, and then those Whoopis would splinter off, and then those other Whoopis too, and it'd be one giant Breck commercial. We'd be all over the fucking planet, and I would never be able to keep track of who the true Whoopi really was, and what she stood for in the first place.

So this way is better, I guess. Until I come up with something else, this is the way to go. You can all stay put for the next while, and bounce off me and give me shit to think about, and laugh about, and care about. Just don't piss me off any more than you have to.

EGGS

I'VE ALWAYS KNOWN what I wanted, and what I liked. I knew early on that I didn't like eggs, that I would never like eggs. I didn't like the way eggs looked. I didn't like the way they smelled. I didn't like what they represented. I mean, what's an egg but a potential chicken? Who the fuck wants to eat potential chicken? If I want chicken, I'll eat chicken.

I should probably state for the record that I support eggs. I endorse them. I like eggs for other people. I don't want the egg people to come after me and say I'm putting down their product. There're probably some chicken lobbyists, somewhere, itching to brand me as evil. So eggs are fine. They're just not for me.

As a kid, I didn't care how you dressed 'em up. An egg was an egg. I couldn't stand that big yellow eye in a fried egg. Scrambled eggs looked like slop. If there was an egg in the egg cream, I wouldn't drink it. If there was that little yellow flaky egg shit in the fried rice from the Chinese takeout, I'd pick it out. I'm sure there were eggs in the cake batter my mother mixed, but I never knew about it. They weren't *clearly* there, and if the cake was yellow my mom could say it was lemon. I liked dippin' eggs at Easter time, and drawing on them, but as soon as you took them out of their little houses I was gone.

One morning when I was about seven, I came to the table for breakfast and there, on my plate, was a scrambled egg. Now, my mother knew I hated the whole idea of eggs, but she decided I should try them. She was like that little Sam-I-Am guy in *Green Eggs and Ham,* and I was gonna try this scrambled egg and open my mind to something new. This was her plan.

My mother didn't understand picky eating. My brother ate everything. Eggs. Corrugated tin. Put it in front of him and he would eat it. My mother too. So she was always on me to try new things, but I was tough. It had to be the right color and the right consistency. If it didn't look right, I wasn't putting it in my mouth, and eggs didn't look right. Just looking at them made me gag, you know. I'd get that egg smell and my throat would close up and I knew I could never eat one. I knew it'd make me puke.

But there I was, in my little school uniform, with my white blouse and plaid jumper and little shoes and socks. My hair was braided. I was ready to go to school. And there on my plate was this thing. This potential chicken. I looked at my mother as if to say, "What are you, crazy?"

"Caryn," she said, "you need to taste them before you can decide not to eat them." She was pleasant enough about it, but she was firm.

I refused. It didn't occur to me that I was defying my mother. I just knew I couldn't swallow that fucking thing. Not even one teeny, tiny bite. Not one iota of egg would I eat. The egg sat there. I sat there. My mother sat there. It was a regular standoff, and I wasn't budging. I was not about to eat that egg. I thought I'd made my position clear. I didn't want to disappoint my mother or cause any trouble, but the thought of eating that egg was too much. It wasn't gonna happen. And so we sat there.

At some point during all this sitting, my mother said I wasn't gonna get anything else to eat until I took a bite of this scrambled egg. Just one bite. It wasn't meant as a threat so much as an incentive. This was how it was. She said it was for my own good. She said it was important to try new things, and I suppose from her perspective it was. From mine, it was important to stay away from eggs, no matter what, but I couldn't get my mother to see my point. So I sat there.

Finally, she sent me off to school, but when I came home that egg was still waiting for me on the table. There were no snacks, no nothing. The egg was supper, but I still wasn't biting. When I woke up the next morning, the egg was still there. At this point, I would have probably gotten botulism, or whatever the fuck people get when they eat eggs that've been left out for too long, but for all I knew my mother was guarding against this possibility and fixing up a new plate every time I stepped into the kitchen. I didn't care. I wasn't giving in. The egg was still there after school that second day, and for supper again the second night, and I started to wonder if I'd ever get anything to eat around my house again. But I didn't care.

See, I wasn't a big eater anyway, so the thought of not eating didn't really bother me. Even today, I don't get particularly hungry, but I know I have to eat. My mother said if there was a big old war or something, then I'd be hungry. I wanted to tell her *she* was the one who'd be hungry, because *I'd* be used to not eating. But when you're seven, you can't say that shit to your mother.

After two days, my mother backed down. She was very smart—smart enough to realize that I truly disliked eggs and wasn't about to try one, no matter what. She didn't say anything about it, though. I just came to the table and the egg was gone and life was back to normal.

She understood. It took her a while, but she understood that this really was a connected thing on my part, that I really had an aversion to eggs, that I wasn't just being flighty. She understood that I would never eat it, that her scrambled egg would still be sitting there to this day if she had held her ground.

This stands now as one of my mother's best lessons on parenting. She didn't realize it, but she taught me that you have to know when to back down. She taught me that sometimes the kid knows. You can't get into a power struggle with a kid, because the kid is always gonna lose. It can't be about power, because you have the power, so you have to be big enough to say, "Okay, I trust you on this. If it turns out you're wrong and you find out down the line that I was right, all the better. But, for now, this is where you're at."

And at forty-one, I'm still in the same fucking place. No egg has passed these lips. And no egg ever will.

SPACE

MALLS TEND TO FREAK ME OUT. I don't understand them. I didn't grow up with them, but they're a part of our landscape now, part of our legacy. It's very strange, you know. I'm a city kid. If you need a head of lettuce or a quart of milk, you go down to the corner to pick it up. If you need a pair of shoes, or a newspaper, you go down the block the other way. Or maybe you have to hop a bus or a subway, or hail a cab, but everything's right there.

In Los Angeles—hell, in most places outside New York—you've got to drive. You can't put your hand out and hail a cab, because they don't have cabs the way we do in Manhattan. You've got to call them up. You can put your hand out, but it won't get you anywhere.

So people get into their cars and drive to these huge concrete structures, even if it's just to pick up some socks, or maybe a card for someone's birthday. Even if you're just going to the movies, you've got to go to the mall. In every city, in every suburb, in every remote town in the middle of nowhere, there's a mall. You go from the darkness of the parking garage right into the store. You never have to go outside.

The parking lots always get me. You never just drive up and pull into a waiting spot, right out front. Remember *Batman,* when they pulled the Batmobile right up to the curb in front of City Hall and hopped out to see Commissioner Gordon? They never had to double-park, or drive around the block to look for a space. There was always a space waiting. In the real world, you roam the parking lot for a decent space, and sometimes you wait for a better space because maybe it's a couple feet closer to the door, and then maybe you linger a bit longer in your space than you need to before giving it up to the next guy because, you know, you had to wait for it, and it's yours. You make the other guy wait just because you can, just because you have the POWER!!!

Power. That's what it comes down to. There's probably a little gene or something in the corners of our brains that leaves us thinking, Why should you just drive up and get this spot? I had to wait, so your ass is gonna wait. It's a territorial thing. We're so powerless in so many other areas of our lives that when we get control of this one little space it goes to our heads. We get to decide someone's future. We get to play God. Does the guy in the Honda Civic get your space, or the guy in the Porsche? The guy in the Porsche doesn't need it. Let him drive around, because he's got enough money to afford a Porsche, so let him valet-park. You're gonna back out to the left, to block out Mr. Porsche, and leave a path for Mr. Honda to slide right in, because he's like you. A bond is formed between you and Mr. Honda against the rich asshole in the Porsche. But then, you know, maybe Bill Gates is behind the wheel of the Honda, so you never fucking know.

You see it all the time. With me it's like, if you're making too much noise or trying to rush me, I will take a lot longer to move. Lean on your horn and I'll slow down. Sometimes people will come up right behind you and they won't get out of your way. They'll honk at you, and yell at you, but they've pulled up in such a way that you're boxed in. What the hell is that? I'll get out of the car and say, "Do you see where your bumper is? How do you expect me to move?" Usually what happens is the guy just gets sheepish and backs up, but sometimes they need to tell you what a sonofabitch you are. They don't get that they're the problem. Yelling at me is not gonna help. Honking is not gonna help. Believe me, honey, it's not gonna help. Just chill out and figure what you're gonna do or go look for another space, because I'm gonna take my time and do what I have to do and whoever gets my spot gets my spot. That's it.

We're running out of room on this planet, that's what it is. That's the problem right there. You look at what people pay for an apartment in Manhattan, and it can be a great apartment, three thousand square feet, a view of the park, twenty-four-hour doormen, but ultimately it's just a box in the sky and we pay buckets of money for the privilege of living in it. It's all about carving out some room for ourselves, and not just any room will do. There are certain areas of space that you want to live in and certain areas of space that you don't want to live in. You're marked by where you live. This neighborhood is good, but this next neighborhood, the next one over, well, it just isn't as good. My space on this block is hipper than your space on the other block. My parking spot is closer to the mall than yours. My seat at the Knicks game is on the floor, and you're up there in the nosebleed section. My apartment in New York is at the center of fucking everything, and that's what I pay for. You take the same apartment and drop it down in the middle of Someplace Else and you'd have to pay *me* to live in it.

It's a simple equation: The more people there are, the less space there is. The more people there are who want the same thing, the less there will be to go around. Look at how many people walk through Central Park on a nice spring day. It's a big park, but it's not big enough. If every New Yorker with a dog and a Frisbee decided at the same time to head out to the park, there'd be a riot. People'd be banging each other on the heads with their Frisbees and the lawyers would clean up. We all live to beat the crowd. We get on line early for the movies, call ahead for reservations, make our last couple calls from the car phone so we can beat the rush-hour traffic home. We're always jockeying for position, looking for the best angle, trying to beat the guy next to us for that last available parking spot.

Now, my view on all this is a little skewed. My sense of personal space is limited. People see me and they come up real close and get in my face. I want to say, "Look, could you back it up a little bit? I see you. You're in my face, how can I not see you?" But I can't always do that without pissing someone off, so I try to be nice about it.

The trick, I think, is to give each other the space we want for ourselves. We move about in this closed, finite environment, where everybody's territory is marked off, and this goes here and that goes there, and we crowd ourselves into these few public areas trying to accomplish whatever it is we need to accomplish. But the world would be a more decent place—wouldn't it?—if we all just chilled a little bit, if we pulled back and gave each other some room. It wouldn't kill us to walk a couple extra rows to the mall entrance, to wait a beat or two for our immediate gratification, to hold the door open for the lady at the post office. Yeah, if you hold the door open for the lady at the post office it probably means she'll wind up ahead of you on the little snake line they've got set up in there, but so what? Let's just spread out and give each other some room—to breathe, and to think. Let's relinquish our parking spaces when we're done with them, and put our blankets down at the beach so we're not right on top of some other group of people, and wait for the bartender to make eye contact with us before barking out our drink order.

Couldn't hurt.

COST

WE LIVE IN A TIME of no real consequence. Check that: I don't mean we live in an inconsequential time, because there's more shit going on now than at any other time in history, but we're beginning to sink under the weight of all that shit. It has fucked with our shared sense of right and wrong, and the message that's finding our kids is that anything goes as long as they can get away with it.

There's no cause and effect anymore between what people do and what happens next. At the other end of every scandal there's a movie of the week, or a No Excuses jeans ad. The notion that we can all do whatever we can get away with is now a part of our culture. It's everywhere. It's what leaves a mother thinking she can blow away her daughter's competition during cheerleader tryouts, clearing a path for America's next sweetheart. It's why we have metal detectors at the front doors to many of our inner-city schools, why babies get snatched from airports and shopping malls and crowded streets, why drive-by shootings are more common than drive-through restaurants.

We just don't seem to care anymore. We don't seem to care what happens to other people just as they don't seem to care about themselves, and one of the reasons is we've seen everyone else lashing out without getting nailed, so we figure we'll lash out, too, and take our chances. Let's get what we can and deal with whatever we have to deal with later.

Now, the easy counter to this argument is O. J. Simpson. I don't want to get into the specifics of the trial because they've been discussed into the ground. What's useful here, though, is to look at the consequences of the Simpson case. O.J.'s not rotting away in jail, where many folks think he should be, or on death row, but he's got no money, no prospects, no respect in his community. Shit, if it turns out the man is, in fact, *not* guilty, he's ruined anyway. There's no place for him to go and get his reputation back, and his kids are gonna grow up knowing what other people think he did to their mother, and his whole life is bent and broken and beyond fixing. I'm surprised the man ever leaves the house. I'm surprised he hasn't climbed back into that fucking Bronco and driven it off a cliff.

It's like the guy down in Atlanta, the so-called Olympic Bomber. For weeks, this guy was on the cover of everything, and no one ever called him the "alleged" bomber. Fuck alleged. He *was* the guy, case closed. And when he was no longer the guy, he was screwed. He should've been on the cover of everything all over again, only this time the headline should have been JESUS CHRIST, WE MADE A MISTAKE, HOW CAN WE POSSIBLY MAKE IT UP TO YOU? But that didn't happen. Of course, they never could have made it up to him, but they could have at least tried. The corrections and retractions were buried in the back of the newspapers, or choked over by newsreaders at the bottom of their broadcasts. The dual message out of this one was that there are sometimes consequences when there's no evidence against you, and that we're screwed either way, but the lesson should have been that even our most cherished institutions—the media, the criminal-justice system, the court of public opinion—sometimes screw up royally.

Then there was that whole special edition of *Newsweek*, on babies and infants, and somehow they put in that it's okay to feed a three-month-old nuts and bolts and razor blades or whatever the fuck it said it was okay to feed 'em. The point is, they fucked up, only the retraction was played more prominently in other publications than it was in *Newsweek* itself. In *Newsweek* it was just a box, and a correction, and a promise to recall the few copies that remained on the stands, but everywhere else it was, Ha, ha, they fucked up; we're glad it wasn't us. *Newsweek* should've had the admission on its own damn cover: We fucked up; put away those nuts and bolts and feed the kiddies strained carrots after all, because, you know, what's more important, saving kids or saving face?

Out in California, there was a nifty scandal at the *San Jose Mercury News*, where reporters came up with a story implicating the CIA in local drug trafficking. It was a sensational story, but when it turned out to be a bullshit story the paper did a full-blown investigation of its own fact-checking procedures, to let the public see where the editors dropped the ball. And they ran it on the front page! How unusual! How wonderful! How brave!—that the editors there were more committed to the pursuit of truth and objective information than they were to covering their own asses.

This last point is the message we need to drive home to young people, and to reflect on ourselves. It was driven home to me as far back as I can remember, and it took. My mother was a big neat freak. I could never leave the apartment until I had my room cleaned the way she liked it. That was the understanding, and for the most part I kept up my end. When I was a kid, you did what you were told. It was a time of "Yes, ma'am"—not "Yes, but . . ."

Once in a while, though, something came up, like when I was about eight and planning to meet up at Lincoln Center with some theater group to see *The Nutcracker*. I was big into that sort of thing, and my mother was cool about letting me go off to a show, or the movies, or wherever, as long as I did my chores. The deal was if I did what she wanted, she would most times let me do what I wanted. I was a good kid, and fairly independent. She knew she could trust me. If I wanted to check something out, she usually let me check it out. "Caryn," she said this one afternoon, "before you go, clean up your room." Which I took to mean, you know, "Before I get back, clean up your room."

Now, I wasn't a dirty kid, but my shit was everywhere. Whenever I straightened my room, I'd look back and wonder how that fucking cyclone managed to sneak in the door when I wasn't looking. Holy shit! Would you look at that! I couldn't keep it neat for trying, but she had me trying. She'd come in for an inspection, and I'd pull the sheet down over the mess, so she couldn't see it. She must've known, and appreciated the effort, because most times she let it slide.

So off she went, to wherever she was going, and I looked at my room, and then I looked at the clock, and then I thought, Hmmmm. I was cutting it pretty close to curtain time. Then the little Whoopi angel popped up on my right shoulder, and the little Whoopi devil popped up on my left shoulder, and they had it out.

The Whoopi devil: "We'll be home before she gets back. Let's go see *The Nutcracker*. Fuck it."

The Whoopi angel: "No, no. Let's clean the room first. You gave your word."

They went back and forth, until finally I plucked the Whoopi angel off my shoulder and went with the devil. You know, why not? I went to hook up with my group, and I sat and watched *The Nutcracker* and it was fabulous. I was in complete awe, and if I thought about my mother at all, or my room, I just figured I'd deal with it when I got home. She wasn't due back until about five o'clock, and I'd be home way before that. I had it covered. All was right with the world.

But then I got home and reached into my pocket for the key to our apartment and came up empty. I had it when I left—I needed it to lock the door—but it was just gone. I frantically searched all my pockets. I even took off my shoes and turned 'em upside down to see if maybe the key was in there. Nothing. I started to panic. I played back the afternoon in my head, trying to find the moment where I and the key parted company. Maybe I'd dropped it on the bus, but there was no way I could trace my steps back to that very same bus and do a search. Maybe it fell out when I was digging in my pockets for some change at Lincoln Center, but I didn't have time to race back uptown to look and still get back before my mom.

And so I panicked some more. I could actually feel my asshole tighten. I started sweating. It was late, past the time I could get the housing authority people to let me in. I looked out the window of our sixth-floor hallway. There were no fire escapes. It wasn't like you could just climb out and open the window, but I started thinking crazy things. I started thinking maybe I could slip out a friend's window and kinda shimmy to one of ours. You know. I was into damage-control mode. If only there was a way into the apartment, there was still time to straighten my room before my mother got home. But there was no way in. My brother wasn't home. The neighbors weren't home. Shit, there was no one around. The whole street seemed empty. The cars stopped moving. Everything just stopped.

Just then, as I was looking down on the street from the hallway window, I caught my mother turn the corner and head my way. I swear, it was as if her eyes zoomed in and locked on mine, and right away, she knew. I felt it in my bones. She was a full block away, but somehow she knew I'd ducked out on my word and gone to Lincoln Center without cleaning my room, and now I was waiting outside our apartment, about to be found out. She knew.

I stood by the elevator and waited for her to come up, and when she did, I could see her face slowly fill the little square window of the elevator door. It was like adjusting the horizontal hold on an old television set and watching the picture reach up to fill the screen, and when my mother's face filled the window, her eyes were still locked on mine. Oh, she definitely knew! By this time, the water was just cascading off my face, my underarms, everywhere. There was no reason for some of these glands to be working, I was only eight, but they just kicked in. I was shaking. I knew I'd fucked up, and I knew I was gonna get it.

"Hello, Caryn," my mother said, stepping from the cab. She knew, but she was stringing me along. I tried to get into the apartment ahead of her, maybe buy myself some time, but she saw right through me.

"What's wrong?" she said. "Something the matter?"

"No," I said. "Nothing. Nothing's wrong."

"How was *The Nutcracker*?"

"Fine. Great. Wonderful."

This took up about five seconds, but it played out like five years. Jesus. In my head, I was moving like I was on speed, and my mother had slowed to like 16 rpm. Remember those old records, the ones slower than 33⅓? In my head, she sounded like an old record played at a too-slow speed.

She opened the door, but I couldn't slink around her. I couldn't get over her. I couldn't get under her. She had taken on the size of the entire apartment. She was gigantic. Every time I tried to zip into my room to close the door, she grew another five feet and filled my path. She crossed to the closet and took off her coat, slowly; it looked like a giant tarpaulin, about to smother me. Then she asked the magic question: "Did you clean your room?"

I went bone dry. Every little ounce of sweat disappeared. It's like the sweat said, Uh-oh, trouble. We're not coming out.

"Yes." It was the Whoopi devil. I wished like hell the fucking angel could have piped in with the truth, but there was no way to take it back.

My mother was pretty good at knowing when I was full of shit. She'd say the color drained from my face, and I'm pretty dark to begin with, so when the color drained from my face, it was pretty fucking obvious.

"You cleaned your room?" my mother said, making sure.

I shook my head, yeah. I tried to get it to go from side to side, but it kept moving up and down. Yeah.

Then she walked down the hall, looked in the room, looked back at me, and shook her head, and in that moment I knew I was the greatest disappointment in my mother's life. That was it, the low point of my daughtering career. Not because I didn't do what I was supposed to do, but because I lied, because I told a stupid little lie that was easier for her to disprove than it was for me to fabricate. Up to that point, it had been about defying my mother, not lying to her, and in my eight-year-old head there was a big difference.

She kicked my butt. It was one of the only times she took a hand to me, and she gave it to me good, and in the middle of it she told me why. She didn't care that I hadn't cleaned my room. I mean, she cared, but not enough to kick my butt. Enough to punish me, but not to kick my butt. No, she whooped me because I told a stupid lie, because I insulted her intelligence, because I shamed myself. And I sat there, taking my beating, and I thought, Okay, Caryn, you did this to yourself. This is not your mom kicking your butt, this is your doing.

It was such a large lesson to me, to be made to stand up and accept the blame for something I'd done. I couldn't lay it on anyone else. It wasn't the Whoopi devil and it wasn't the Whoopi angel. It was me. It was my sorry fucking shiftless ass. Once I fucked up, I should've just copped to it and said, "Yeah, I didn't get it done." Or, "I chose not to do it." I should have just taken the consequences, but I tried to snake my way out of it with a stupid lie.

Kids don't lie to cover their tracks, or their ass; they lie because they panic, because they can't think what else to do. There's no strategy to it. It's an act of desperation. That was how it was with me. I lied for no good reason. I was desperate. I panicked. It wasn't the first time I lied to cover my own ass, but it was the first time I got caught—and the last time I tried. If you're gonna fuck up, then fuck up, but cop to it, own it, learn from it, and move on. Take the fucking consequences. What's that shit they teach you in physics? For every action there's an equal and opposite reaction? Well, accept it. Wait for it. If you set a thing in motion, you know it's gonna come back to bite you at the other end. You just know. Don't come up with a chickenshit lie, or talk your way out of it, or hire a fancy-ass lawyer to keep justice at the door, because in the end you'll be found out and you'll just make it worse. I'm not into this notion that there's some higher power, keeping score, and that when your day of reckoning comes He will find some way to even things up. That's bullshit. The only higher power you have to worry about is everyone else. It's you and me, honey. It's the rest of us. We'll catch on, sooner or later. We're not as stupid as you think, and you're not as smart as you think. Cover your ass and we will find you, and we will make you pay. If not now, then later. But soon.

My mother taught me that.

CHEER

CHRISTMAS WAS IT around our house. The high point, the focal point, the main point. It sometimes seemed it was the point of the whole fucking show, and it surprised the shit out of me every year.

We had the drill down. My mom would come home with the tree. Nothing special, just a tree, and she'd put the tree in that little tree holder thing and tighten it up so it stood straight. She'd leave it up for a few days, maybe a week or so, and it'd just be standing there, all bare and good-smelling, and I'd come home from school and hang up my jacket and look around to see if there were any presents underneath it, or if anything had magically materialized around it during the day. But there was never anything under the tree. It was just bare, and waiting.

Still, I'd look, and breathe in that wonderful real Christmas-tree smell, and try to imagine what was coming. That smell always got me. Even today, I have to have that sweet pine mixed with the juicy aroma of our slow-cooking turkey, which my mother used to put in about nine o'clock on Christmas Eve. Give me that smell on Christmas, honey, and I'm set.

Finally, one night pretty close to Christmas, we'd start in with the lights and circle the tree. It was just me and my mom and my brother. Sometimes there was my cousin, but usually it was just the three of us, which was how it was the rest of the time anyway, so, you know, that was cool. Our Christmas-tree lights were red and green and orange and yellow, and they'd flick on and off. We used the same lights every year. We couldn't go buying new stuff. We had our lights and we were set. We also had the string with the liquid bubbling up inside the lights, and we'd circle the tree with that too, and then we'd rip open a new package of tinsel, and run and tear and toss the tinsel. The tinsel you couldn't keep from one year to the next; you had to buy new stuff. We did our Isadora Duncan moves, and we got that shit up on the tree in all kinds of configurations. Next came the peppermint candy canes, then the liquid snow they used in department-store windows. We'd spray the snow on the windows at an angle, so it looked like it had built up from being blown against the panes by the wind.

Sometimes we'd write "Merry Christmas" on the windows with a stencil and a rag dipped in pink window cleaner, or do up a picture of a reindeer. You'd dot the rag around and, just like that, you had a reindeer on your window.

This all happened in one night. From bare tree to a done-up department-store window took just a couple hours. We'd have the Christmas music going, or if the decorating ran into Christmas Eve, maybe we'd have the television tuned to the yule log broadcast on

Channel 11, for the background music. We'd never actually sit and *watch* the yule log, because even we knew that was kinda cheesy, but we'd listen and put all the stuff on the tree and laugh and laugh and laugh. It was the most delicious time. There were still no presents under the tree, but we knew Mom was just waiting for us to go to sleep.

Finally, when the decorations were through, we'd watch *A Christmas Carol,* the British version, the one with Alastair Sim, which for my money is the only one to watch. We'd all gather in front of our black-and-white television set for the last piece of the routine. After the movie, we'd go to bed. I still watch that sucker every Christmas Eve, and I still go to bed right after. I need Alastair Sim and the smell of the tree and the turkey, else Christmas ain't really happening for me, you know.

In the middle of the night, my brother used to wake me up with a tap on the shoulder and take me into the living room. He was all, "Shhhhhh, Caryn, shhhhhh," until I was all the way awake, then I was the one shushing him. It was a small apartment, just two rooms. It was tough to move about without attracting attention. Mom sometimes slept in the living room, but on some nights she doubled up with me, so we never really knew if we'd be found out on our midnight run. I'm sure she knew. She had to know. We were giggling too much for her not to know. But she never stirred. We were about as quiet as two kids could be, banging into things and shit, but she never stirred.

I remember coming down our darkened hallway, and turning the corner into the living room, and seeing the reflection of the lights on the walls. On and off, and on and off. Man, it was an enchanted fucking sight. The apartment lights were all out, but the Christmas tree was lit up like Vegas. It was the main strip, right there; it was like the room had been dipped in all the colors of the rainbow. On and off, and on and off.

And then—there it was. My brother, Clyde, and me, we never tired of the game. We never knew how Mom got all those presents underneath the tree in that small apartment without our noticing. We could never figure out where her hiding places were, or when, exactly, she jumped into action. It was one of the wonderments of our growing up, but there'd always be these great presents, like a bicycle, or skates, or whatever we were into that year. All the things a kid could possibly want for Christmas were laid out under our tree, all beautifully wrapped and waiting for our greedy little paws to tear them open. It'd just knock us out. I never had any idea how she even afforded it, forget the logistical problem of getting the stuff wrapped and under the tree undetected. But we had to hurry back into bed before Mom caught us. We couldn't open the presents until morning, and even then we couldn't open them until after breakfast. We'd be jumping up and down, shouting "Merry Christmas!" over and over, but we'd have to polish off our Maypo before we could do anything about it.

We'd bring out our little gifts for each other. I was big into these little perfumes for my mom, or some scarves. Basically anything I could get at the five-and-ten for not a whole lot of money that was kinda nice. I'd collect the Hoffman soda bottles and trade them in for nickels, and I'd usually have some money left over from my birthday, which was back in November. I'd buy my brother some socks, or a book, and that was about as far as my money went, but that was enough.

If there was snow, we'd head out to play. We'd get on Clyde's Flexible Flyer and sled down Tenth Avenue. Remember those serious snowstorms? We don't get them much anymore, but back then, the city would just shut down and Tenth Avenue became the Alps. My brother would push me from behind. He'd run and run and run and push and push and push and then finally hop on. He'd be yelling in my ear, "Hold on, Caryn. Hold on." Or he'd be tellin' me to lean this way or that way. Now, there wasn't much of a pitch to Tenth Avenue, but if the snow was packed just right and you got a good run going, you could slide forever. He'd make like I was a bad driver, and that I was gonna hit a parking sign or something, and he'd holler and laugh. Whenever we came to a stop I'd look up from my laughing and say, "Do it again." That was the line, "Do it again." And Clyde would grab the rope he had tied to the front of the sled and pull me back up the street for another ride.

Christmas was one of the best times of all in our house, with the tree and the turkey and the three of us. Just the best. And not because we were celebrating the birth of Christ. That wasn't what it was about for me. It was a seasonal thing, a ritual, something to look forward to. It was the ticking off of another year. It was looking outside and finding a fresh snowfall to surpass the one we'd sprayed on the window the night before, which happened maybe once or twice but somehow has become part of the memory.

Christmas feels the same way to me now, as an adult, and I look forward to it for the same childish reasons—for the presents, for the tree, for the way we can all be together, for the sheer fucking surprise of it. I don't know if it means anything, but it's not important to me if it means anything. Me and organized religion, we don't understand each other on a philosophical level. Sentimentally, I'm an easy touch, but philosophically, intellectually, I'm not so sure. It gets me in the heart, but the head's just not so sure. Yeah, I went to Catholic school, and yeah, I had this stuff drummed into me from the very beginning, but in my neighborhood there were too many religions going on to take any one of them too seriously. We had Jews. We had Buddhists. We had Muslims. We had a Greek Orthodox church. Each religion had the same basic guidelines: Be good to people; don't lie; don't screw around with your neighbor's wife; don't hurt anyone unless they're hurting you, and even then you shouldn't really hurt them, unless of course they're *really* hurting you, at which point you should just tear their fucking face off. These are the general rules, and it's all basically the same.

So now I celebrate everything. I consider myself a humanist. I'll even celebrate Kwanza, though I'm not sure I get it. Some people reject it because of the newness of it, because it seems to be a fabrication, but others embrace it as an African tradition. Whatever it is, I'll go ahead and celebrate it because, shit, the holidays are just a time when we can all get together and say, "How the fuck are you?" No matter what. No matter that two months ago I couldn't stand you. I will deal with you during the holidays and maybe make some sort of peace. That's when you put it all aside and try to work things out. You sit, you eat, you talk about good old times. Anyway, you try. That's what Christmas is all about—trying, staying connected, remembering what's important. Don't sell me no line on Jesus Christ, but sit down next to me and tell me how you're doin'. Next week I may not give a shit, but I'll give a shit on Christmas. Hell, maybe I'll give two.

My frame of reference for Christmas will always be back in that apartment in Chelsea. I do up Christmas the same way every time, wherever I am, whenever I can. Same bare tree until the last possible minute, same over-the-top presents, same Alastair Sim before bed. Home is where Christmas is, you know. California Christmases, well . . . it doesn't quite feel the same in the heat, so I try to get back to New York, or to our place up in Connecticut. And once in a while, if we're lucky, we'll catch some snow.

You know what I did? I went out and bought myself a brand-new Flexible Flyer at FAO Schwarz. Jesus, those things are expensive, but they're worth every fucking penny when you've got your big brother staying with you and there's a fresh snow and you drag his ass out of bed and get him to push you from behind and hop on, like when you were kids. Then it doesn't matter what it costs.

FLOCK

MOST MAN-MADE RELIGION is built on fear. This is my theory. The fear of judgment. The fear of retribution. Our fears come in all shapes and sizes. One of my favorites is the fear of other religions, or other ways of thinking, and this one's at the root of all our problems. I mean, what the fuck were the Crusades all about? I am going to kill you in the name of God. Yeah, yeah, I know God said thou shalt not kill, but this thou is gonna kill thine ass anyway, and thou's gonna do it so you'll know you were killed by thou in God's name. That's the deal. In Ireland and England, Israel and Syria, it cuts the same way: My religion is better, I'm right, so I'm gonna kill you. I'm not even gonna discuss it. I'm gonna blow up your shit, because my shit's better than yours and you're doing it all wrong.

Perhaps our most common fear is the fear of fucking up—right?—and it's been with us since the beginning. If you buy into Adam and Eve, you buy into your first fuck-ups. Eve went and bit that apple and nothing's been right since. The first fuck-ups begat a whole group of fuck-ups: Adam, Eve, Cain, Whoopi . . . And now fucking up has become an art form. There are so many things to fuck up, and so many ways to go about it. If it moves, we'll find a way to fuck it up. You can fuck up your relationships, you can fuck up your career, you can fuck up your neighborhood.

I'm a fan of the big J.C., because he wasn't afraid of fucking up. Buddha, Krishna . . . all those cats had it down. They knew the world was not about my shit and your shit. It wasn't about His shit either. Those leaders knew we were all afraid of something. They said, "Look, I'm giving up all my worldly goods, because I don't need anything, and I'm not going to throw stones at you, because I know how tough life is." And there was no scaring them.

The way I see it, the Catholic Church has strayed from what Christ was all about. Me, personally, I've tried to hold fast. It ain't easy, swimming against the current, but I do what I can. I was schooled Catholic, but I don't take a lot of it to heart. I use the basics—do unto others, don't judge unless your own shit is in order—because they make sense. My biggest problem is, I don't like the guy we've got in office. I'm sure he's a nice guy and all, but I'm just not big on Pope John Paul II. I'm sorry, but I can't accept a pope with the audacity to judge as though he were God. He doesn't have the stripes to dismiss homosexuality as an abomination, or to reject abortion or divorce as viable alternatives to fucking up, and it just pisses me off. I thought God was the final judge. Wasn't He the one tellin' us to come to Him, let's talk, we'll work things out? Who the fuck is the pope, to judge people like that? Yeah, he's the pope, but that doesn't give him the right to wipe out what he doesn't accept or understand. It's not up to a pope to accept or reject us. It's not even up to him to forgive us. That goes to a higher authority, you know. That job's taken.

Popedom is not what it was. There have been great popes and not-so-great popes, and to me this current one just checks in at the low end. The pope for me was John XXIII; he was the one. What gets me about him was that no one gave him a thought before he got the gig. He wasn't charismatic. He wasn't known as a leader. Shit, he wasn't known at all. He was just a simple guy, and when the College of Cardinals was split on a successor to Pius XII, they put him up as a way to break the tie. He wasn't supposed to get any votes himself, just move some of the other votes around, but somehow he walked into the job.

The cardinals were in shock, because this was not the man they wanted. But John XXIII was a great pope. The church was full on his watch. He turned night into day. He was a regular fucking godsend. He put himself out there and asked, How can we expect people to stay with the Catholic Church if they don't know anything about us? How can we hold them if we don't talk to them in their language? How can we celebrate people who wrote Psalms to glorify God and at the same time deny our poets the ability to write songs in praise of God now? How can we do this? How can we expect young people to talk to our priests, who have no face in the community except as these pillars of piety, all dressed in black? What are we doing, hiding behind these costumes? We have to bring God's word to the people, because the people aren't coming to us. They just aren't. We have to go into the neighborhoods, and sit with these folks, and help them embrace the choices they've made.

So he made a lot of changes. He made it so the nuns and the priests could wear normal-people clothes and do normal-people things. He made it so they could go down to the schoolyard and play basketball with the kids, or go to dinner in people's homes, or run a soup kitchen. He made it so we could sing songs to God with a backbeat. The people were, like, "Yes, oh, you're a nun. Cool. Love that color on you, honey."

John XXIII made it so you could ask questions and look on God's servants as regular folks. If something was on your mind, you could just put it out there and see what it looked like. You could come into church and sing the folk mass—in English or Spanish or Ukrainian or whatever you wanted. This pope's idea of God was not as some scary, horrible monolith who'd banish you if you pissed Him off. This was a God we could relate to, a God for the huddled masses.

John XXIII reminded us that God gives us choice, and that God forgives. We're just talking *for* Him, he said. You can talk to God wherever you are. You don't need us. You don't need to come into the church. You can find your own long-distance carrier, you know. You can say to God, I made a mistake, and God will forgive you. Man does not have the right to judge you, and God turns His back on no one.

This was the man's message, and I loved him for it. I loved him because there was finally room for mistakes. And for doubt. And discussion. There was room for radical ideas. You could ask if Judas was actually without choice, if it seemed to you that Judas had to do what he did in order for everything else to happen. You could wonder if Joseph was kinda pissed that Mary was pregnant by God. You could ask whatever popped into your little mind, and no one would run you out or dress you down or make you feel ashamed.

And then John XXIII died and everything sort of went to shit, and now we've got ourselves a pope who'd like us all to be back in the fifteenth century. He's not particularly flexible, this John Paul II. He doesn't seem open to other cultures or other ideas, or to accept that God meant us to grow with the world, and change, and do our best. He doesn't get that the church is here to help us. Is he a bad guy? No, I just think he's limited. He's done some wonderful things in terms of trying to educate people about Communism, but to me, the rest of his focus has been off. As far as leading people to God, I don't think he understands it. I don't think the Catholic Church as a whole understands it anymore. I mean, this is one of the richest institutions in the world, but it's built on a cat who didn't hold on to his money, who spread it out among the poor, who made sure the people had what they needed.

Remember the pagan-baby boxes? Those yellow-tan boxes we had to fill with our candy money, for Lent? The boxes had a little picture of an African baby, with bananas around its waist and big red lips and big eyes, and this was supposed to represent the children our money was going to help save. These were the pagan babies of the world, and the missionaries were going to save them for us, with our very own money. We all got into the idea of helping out these children, and at the end of Lent we'd have like six bucks in our boxes and we gave them to the nuns and then we never saw them again. We never got an update. Nothing. The money was just gone, and this was how it went throughout the Catholic Church, which meant that for years and years and years you had these schoolkids giving up their candy money. It adds up. There are still pagan babies in the world, and the Catholic Church pays no money in taxes. Nada. Nothing.

The Catholic Church has more money than God, so I say, Sell a ring. Sell a hat. Sell some property. Sell Paramount Studios. The church owns the sidewalk out front. This is what I hear, and maybe it's bullshit, but what if it's not? What does the church need with a piece of Hollywood sidewalk? Sell some of that shit. Sell the goddamn *Pietà*. You want to stop hunger in Poland, sell the *Pietà,* you know. You want to help out in Bosnia, sell some of those fucking crowns. What are you doing with all that shit anyway? It ain't doing nothing. It ain't making any money. The big J.C. would not dig this at all, man. He wouldn't dig it at all. He'd take one look around and go, "You, out. You, out. You, you, you. Out, out, out." He'd make a clean sweep because this was not what He came here to do. He came to give people hope, and the church right now offers no hope. It just doesn't. It has no humor, no life, no humanity. It's all about politics and commerce, and this makes me sad. It bums me out tremendously, what the church has become, and if it's got *me* bummed, imagine what J.C. must be feeling.

. . .

So now I've gotten to where man-made religion makes no sense to me. If it's meant to frighten us, to stand for something bigger than us, to hold us in line, then it's not meant for me. I don't get it. I think God, or whoever's sitting in that top spot, has much more of a sense of humor than we give Him credit for. And a great sense of irony. Shit, He'd have to have that irony, to roll with what He's had to roll with, but He would not get what's been happening lately. No, He would not get the way His message has been co-opted and corrupted. He would not get this pope, or some of the other yahoos been left minding the store.

Absolutely, He'd be confounded at what's going on. He'd be shouting down on us: "Hey, you down there, what could you possibly be thinking? I cook up this scenario, and I start to think maybe it can turn into something interesting, and then you go and fuck it up. Adam and Eve, you give in to temptation, but then I go back and think, Okay, I'm willing to work with you on temptation. I'll relax the rules a little bit, start to think maybe temptation isn't such a bad thing if I just go back and tinker with the formula, but then you people come up with all kinds of temptations I'd never even considered. You make it hard. It's like one minute I've got my hand on the tiller and then I look up and we've veered so completely off course that I, the creator, can't figure how to right the ship and set us back on our original path.

"And as for you popes, well, you've just muddied things up even further, and I don't get your agenda. I don't get all the jewelry and the property and the pomp. I just don't get it. I don't get the high-mindedness, or the superiority. I don't get that you've become the gatekeepers, and you don't get that if there's gonna be a gate at all it needs to swing open, not closed. What it boils down to is caring for each other, tolerating each other, forgiving each other, helping each other. That's it. Make each other laugh, for My sake. Or go to hell."

LOVE

AIN'T IT GRAND?

RACE

CALL ME AN ASSHOLE, call me a blowhard, but don't call me an African American. Please. It divides us, as a nation and as a people, and it kinda pisses me off. It diminishes everything I've accomplished and everything every other black person has accomplished on American soil. It means I'm not entitled to everything plain old regular Americans are entitled to.

Every time you put something in front of the word *American,* it strips it of its meaning. The Bill of Rights is my Bill of Rights, same as anyone else's. It's my flag. It's my Constitution. It doesn't talk about *some* people. It talks about *all* people—black, white, orange, brown. You. Me.

People who come from other countries and become American citizens deserve everything this country has to offer, so how come I don't? Don't qualify my right to be here among you good people. Don't make it conditional. Who died and made you the fucking maître d'? What's your family name? When did your ancestors come to this country? What language did they speak? How come you're more American than I am? Because it's easier for you to blend in? I'm sorry, but it's just not acceptable. Not anymore.

So, no, I am not an African American. I'm not from Africa. I'm from New York. My roots run a whole lot deeper than most of the people who don't have anything in front of the word *American.* I can trace my family tree back to the *Mayflower.* We may not have been on it, but we were under it, and that counts too. We're out of Florida, for the most part. We're Seminole Indians. We're a couple Jews from Russia. We're black and white. There's even some Chinese running through my blood. They were here to build the railroad, and they stopped to add to my strange mix.

I'm a mutt. There's a whole historical adventure that belongs to me, and I refuse to let our cultural demagogues rob me of what's mine. George Washington belongs to me. Lou Gehrig belongs to me. Jackie Robinson belongs to me. Nathan's hot dogs belong to me. You know. The Lower East Side is mine. The amber waves of fucking grain? Mine. I'm as American as Chevrolet.

For centuries now, people have come to America from all over the world. It wasn't an all-white country up until the time some of the wealthy landowners started importing black folks as chattel, the way some of the supremacists would have us think. Shit, some of our most outspoken black leaders would have us believe the same, but that's crap. We were here. There may have been a slave or two along the line, but for the most part my people were free. Before we were in Florida, we were in Oklahoma, which was a free territory before it became a state. We worked the land. We had jobs. We had property. We had families.

Yeah, people call themselves Irish Americans or Polish Americans or Native Americans, but that just cheapens who they are and what they're about. It might reinforce someone's idea of our origins, and remind them of our ancestors, but it takes away from what we are now. You don't hear any Jews running around calling themselves Jewish Americans. The last time I heard someone referred to as a Catholic American was when Kennedy was president. Rosa Parks did not sit on that bus so that I could put something in front of the word *American.* She sat on the bus to remind people that we are all entitled to the same thing. That's why she was on the bus. She didn't sit on the bus so I could go looking for a mother country. I'm in the fucking mother country.

I've been to Africa, and they look at me and go, "Huh?" We go over there, talking all that brother shit, and they can see we don't have a clue. They're polite enough about it, I suppose, but it's clear we don't understand the culture, or the people, or anything. We don't understand the culture because it's not ours, it's theirs. The Africans don't look at us and accept us as Africans. Maybe they'll consider us distant relatives, but we're not Africans. "You're an American," they'll say. "Why aren't you proud of that? Why aren't you proud of what you've built? That's your country. Look at all you've got. Look how hard you struggled to get it. What the hell's the matter with you?"

There are people I admire a great deal who've embraced the term, but I tell them straight out to leave me alone about it. Call yourself whatever the fuck you want to call yourself, but don't tell me I've got to answer to it. We don't all know each other, and we don't have to agree with each other, and on this one we're on a completely different page.

You know, there's always been a kind of racism within the black community itself. Here it's just about semantics, or a misguided search for a new identity, but a lot of times it's about something as simple as the hue of our skin. We dark-skinned blacks are pissed at the light-skinned blacks because they can pass as white, because they're not black enough, and the light-skinned blacks are pissed at the dark-skinned blacks because we somehow make them feel inferior, you know.

My daughter happens to be very light-skinned, and she had the hardest time as a teenager trying to figure out what she was. I didn't understand it. I thought, Well, what do you mean, what are you? All the time, she'd come up to me and say, "Am I black?" Well, yeah, you're black. Your father's black. I'm black. You're black. But then she'd start in on why she was so light. Well, you're light because your father's light, because there's white people in his family. There's white people in my family. And you throw what you throw. There's no clear black line anywhere in this country. You are what you are.

In truth, though, when you hear people talk about someone being too black, or not black enough, they're talking about attitude. It might seem like they're talking about the color of their skin, but it's the attitude underneath the color that gets people going. None of our first crossover entertainers were particularly light-skinned, although the prevailing myth now is that they were. Nat King Cole wasn't light. Ella Fitzgerald wasn't light. Satchmo. Sammy Davis, Jr. Dorothy Dandridge. Lena Horne—well . . . she was so light the movie studios thought maybe they could pass her off; they used to call her an exotic, to kinda cover their asses and mess with poor Lena's head.

For a long time, people said one of the reasons for Harry Belafonte's huge appeal was that his skin was so light, but I never understood that. I'm sorry, but Harry is just not that light. He's my complexion, maybe just a shade lighter. But you can't mistake Harry for anything other than a black man, and I have a hard time imagining that anyone ever looked at him and thought, Hmmmmm, I wonder . . .

Hattie Winston was the first black person I saw on television in a normal capacity, doing normal, everyday things. She was a wonderful actress, and the first black performer in my frame of reference featured in a mainstream commercial. She was taking a shower, or brushing her teeth, and I saw this and thought, Oh, right, black people do this too. It was a great, great thing to see, a validating thing. It wasn't for a black product. They didn't advertise black products on television until *Soul Train*. It was a giant, race-free blip on the social scale.

And then *Julia* came along, with Diahann Carroll. I was about thirteen when that show came on the air, and to see this beautiful black woman playing a nurse, a single mother whose husband had died in the war, was a real triumph. A black woman who wasn't working as a maid! Who didn't weigh fourteen hundred pounds! Who walked with her head high and her eyes dead ahead! To be represented in a way that was intelligent, and not just playing for laughs, like *Amos 'n' Andy,* you know, was a serious thing. It said, Yeah, we're out here, same as you, trying to raise our kids and do our jobs. Same as you.

I used to do a character, a little black girl who wanted blond hair. Everyone on television was blond and she wanted to be blond. That's what it was like, growing up black in the 1960s. Until *Julia,* there were no black faces on television, no role models working in good jobs or setting positive examples. I'd sit with my mother and wonder about this white woman's hair, or that one's lips, and she'd just look at me and say, "Ain't gonna happen." And she was right. There was no fucking way. They would no sooner wind up looking like me than I'd wind up looking like them.

Now we've got whole networks that have essentially been built on black programming, even though the programming kind of sets us back. Now we're back to the eye-poppin', slang-slingin' shit we used to get from J.J. on *Good Times,* when we should be beyond that. I'm sorry, but Martin Lawrence does not reflect what it means to be black today any more than Beaver and Wally reflected what it meant to be white in 1960.

I sometimes wonder whether the choices I make as a black actress contribute in some way to the prevailing stereotypes, but then I realize it's not all on me. I can take any role I want, or reject any role I want, for any reason I want. Early on in my career, a lot of the scripts I saw called for me to play a maid, or a nanny, and I resisted it at first. I thought I was better than that. But then I thought about it some more and realized that it didn't matter what the character's job was. Since when are we defined by what we do? We're defined by who we are, and if the stories that interest me happen to be about maids and nannies, then that's fine. I didn't give a shit that other black actresses thought it was degrading to have to play a domestic, because they were wrong and I was right. I'm always right.

Still, though, it gnawed at me. I started shooting a movie called *The Long Walk Home,* in Montgomery, Alabama. I was above the title. They weren't paying me a whole lot of money, but I was above the title, and I walked through the first few days of shooting thinking, If I'd been from this era, I'd have done this, and I'd have done that. This was just a part. I'd do it like it was written, for the movie, but I needed to know how I would have done it for real.

And then I started talking with some of the black women from the area, the women who worked as maids and nannies, who swallowed their pride and did what they had to do to raise their families and carry on. They sat me down and set me straight. "Look," one of them said, "you wouldn't have done it any differently. You just have a different sensibility. The world is a different place. When we were coming up, if you made any noise, they'd hang you. No questions asked. They'd come in the middle of the night, and they'd take your family, and they'd kill you."

She was right. I was wrong. (So maybe I'm not *always* right.) You had to find ways to do what you did and stay alive. And it hadn't occurred to me. It hadn't been my experience. I'd never lived with the threat that if I spoke my mind someone would break into my house in the dead of night and take my child and cover him with hot tar and feathers and hang him in a tree. It never occurred to me because I didn't know our own history. Most of us don't know our own history. That's why, every February, I turn on the news and get myself a bit of Black History Month. We just get a month, and it's the smallest month they've got, but we've been through some important shit. There's more to us than George Washington Carver and the fucking peanut. We couldn't vote in a lot of the country until 1963. In my lifetime, we couldn't fucking vote. This is astonishing to me, and these women from Montgomery helped to bring the point home. I started to look on them as heroic. They raised a lot of kids, white and black, who've gone on to do great things. They held their breath and their tongue until the world caught up to what was right. They kept the family together—theirs, and the upper-class white families they were working for. And they survived. So what the hell was wrong with playing them? Nothing. Nothing.

As a kid in New York, I wasn't raised with the idea that we were anything but New Yorkers. I'm not conditioned, when someone walks into a room, to think to myself, Oh, he's white, or, Oh, he's black. It's not important. I mean, where do you go from there? What does that mean? You still don't know anything about that person, you can't get beyond it. Yeah, I remember when there was an effort to integrate into the larger community, and to broadcast it out to other people, but that time has passed. We're here. We've been here a long fucking time, and made vital contributions to this country. Without black people, we would have been a lot slower walking into a lot of the shit we walked into. The Industrial Revolution would have been a lot longer in coming. The Information Age would have taken its time. We helped, and that's why I refuse to be labeled an African American. When you tell the story of this country, I'm part of the fabric. Black people, stop trying to identify elsewhere. This is yours. People in the South got their legs chewed off, got hit with fuckin' fire hoses, got their children blown up, got yanked, burned, hanged, and sliced so that you wouldn't have to pretend you were from someplace else. So that you wouldn't have to say, "No, I'm not entitled to this." Well, fuck that. You're entitled to all of it. Take it. It's ours.

SEX

I WAS ONCE MARRIED to a guy who couldn't give head to save his life. I was busting to tell him, "Get a Life Saver and put your tongue through it, motherfucker. That's all you gotta do."

Ask. Experiment. If you want to be a good partner, the kind your bitter ex won't mind paying off with a million-dollar divorce settlement, you've got to be open to new ideas. It's never too early to start. Play around down there. See what happens. Figure out what feels good, and when, and why. And keep at it.

When I was younger I tried to go down on myself, with some success. I actually could reach, and I remember thinking that was a big deal, but I couldn't do much down there. I could get to it, but that wasn't enough. You have to be double-jointed and flexible and big into yoga if you want to get anything accomplished. I couldn't really get off on just reaching. A lot of people have probably tried. (Shit, I hope so; I just admitted I tried to eat myself out when I was a kid, so y'all better be fallin' in line right behind me.) I think guys have it easier, because their dicks are reaching back in the other direction; they're helping out a little bit. It's easier to get to dick than pussy, if it's your dick or your pussy. And with pussy you not only have to get down there, you have to kind of get down and around and underneath. You have to be able to see what you're doing, get a feel for the area, spend some time with it, only with me it was just too fucking uncomfortable to keep at it. I was all curled and rolled into a ball and craning my neck like a long-necked dinosaur in the fetal position.

I'm sure there are some people out there who can jerk themselves off orally without too much trouble, and without looking too ridiculous. Good for them. Really. It's like that old joke about why dogs like to lick their balls—because they can. Well, if you can, do. Go for it. I can't imagine, though, that there are too many guys out there willing to swallow their own come. No fucking way. That's always a big thing with guys, whether or not you swallow, but I'm thinking it should be put up or shut up, you know. If you're not gonna kiss me right afterward, or put your tongue in my mouth, then why the fuck do I have to swallow that shit? Tell me. You can't even deal with secondhand come, or you freak out if it gets in your hair or on your clothes, and you expect us to swallow whatever you can produce of the real deal. So no way is there a heterosexual guy out there sucking himself off and swallowing his own come. No way.

We all do "feel good" things to ourselves, or to our partners, and that's cool as long as we're all consenting adults about it. Whatever feels good, you know. But we shouldn't limit feeling good to adults.

Parents get all weird when they catch their kids trying to feel good, and I don't understand that. It's a natural thing. They're not hurting anybody. They can deal with their little boys pulling their puds, 'cause it's kinda cute. Those tiny penises look like little gnome-things, with their little hats, sitting on two tiny rocks. But it's not so cute when it's a little girl, rubbing up against her pillow. When they catch their little girls it's, *Oh, no, this is not good.* They shoo our little hands away, because if they didn't they fear we'd be down there all the time. And they're right, we would. (We are.) It may take us a little longer to find it and figure out how it works, but once we get it, we get it. Wait a minute. What is this. Oh. Yeah. That. Oooooh.

We still carry a lot of fucked-up Puritan baggage about sex in general, and about masturbation in particular, and it all gets in the way of what we should be teaching our kids. Former Surgeon General Joycelyn Elders took a lot of shit for suggesting masturbation should be taught in the schools, but what's wrong with that? People lit into ol' Joycelyn for saying masturbation was a viable way for young people to experiment sexually without the risk of infection or pregnancy, but it is. It should be talked about in school, and at home. If we're gonna tell our kids to abstain from sexual intercourse, or to think pretty damn hard before having sexual intercourse, then we owe them some alternatives. They need to know what else they can be doing, and how they can go about doing it.

With boys, I guess this would be what they call a gut class. There wouldn't be too much in the way of new material. Pull, pull, pull. Rub, rub, rub. It's basic. But a girl, you know, she might need pointers, some direction. She'll need to know that she should go home and make an okay sign with her fingers, and insert her pointer finger and feel around until the room gets fuzzy and that'll mean she's found her spot. Once she's found it, she can touch that spot any time she wants. She can still make out with her boyfriend and have all those wonderful feelings and then go home and touch that spot. Boys are born knowing what to do, but girls need to be told. Absolutely, they need to be told.

Honey, this is one time you won't hear students bitchin' about their homework. Shit, they'll be lining up for extra credit, and we've got to find new and responsible ways of giving it to them. And why stop with masturbation? While we're at it, let's teach 'em how to do it to each other too. (The better students can maybe graduate to going down on each other.) Let's teach the boys that girls are all built differently, that our clitorises are not always in exactly the same place, that sometimes they're really tiny and sometimes they're gigantic, that you have to figure out how much pressure to put on them and how much pressure not to put on them. Let's remind the girls that an erect penis comes with ammunition, you know, that when she strokes her boyfriend and it feels good he's gonna send out a little thank-you note. She needs to be ready for that.

For a long time, I was a big advocate of oral sex for young people. I used to tell kids, my own included, that if they wanted to experiment this was a good way to go. It was kinda like safe sex, except it was a little bit out there and racy and exciting. It's also a good way to learn about hygiene, and keeping yourself clean for the benefit and enjoyment of another person, but now there are so many diseases running around out there that I've stopped pushing people in that direction. There'll be plenty of time for that later.

Our sexual revolutions are everywhere. I came through a time when people were fucking on the street. You could have a group fuck in Central Park with people you didn't even know, and then go home and think nothing of it. But times have changed. There's a new revolution. For me, I now want to be with someone I can talk to. I don't like one-night stands. They don't have the same oomph they once had. I don't know that I was ever truly comfortable with the concept of casual sex, or sport fucking, but now there are just too many ways to die, if you're not careful. Diseases, psychopaths . . . who the fuck knows what's out there? So you have to know the people you're having sex with. Have some idea.

I work with a group in Los Angeles called Covenant House, and what they're finding, frighteningly, is that more and more kids over the age of thirteen are coming in and testing positive for HIV. It's like a boom. For all the cautionary messages we're putting out there, the truth is just not sinking in. Or maybe it is, and these kids just don't care. Maybe they're not paying good attention, or think they're indestructible, or that these bad things are happening to some other group of young people. Maybe they just need the comfort of holding another person, and they haven't been taught that there are ways of holding another person without it leading to sex. They find themselves in positions of need and then they turn up ill. They don't understand that sex is no longer something you just jump up and do. They don't get that there should be a buildup to it, that if you're going to have multiple partners you have to take certain precautions.

But maybe this latest revolution has spun us back around to the right place. Maybe sex should never have been something we just jumped up and did. Maybe all those group fucks in Central Park got us thinking the wrong way. A lot of people wonder how much it sucks, for people coming of age in the time of AIDS, to have their first sexual experiences tainted by an unknowable disease, to have to worry that what feels good might kill them, or fuck up their lives so completely they'll forever kick themselves for their impulses, or for what they've missed. But what if it doesn't suck? What if this is a good thing, or at least not such a bad thing? What if there's a silver lining to what seems like a raw deal? We've gone from where it was nothing to fuck another person to where it's now everything. And maybe that's okay.

When I started messin' with it, sex wasn't about talking. It wasn't about connecting in some real, substantial way. It was about getting your rocks off. It was about defying authority and flaunting your freedom and not getting caught. But we've gotten away from that, and we now need to connect to the people we're fucking, whether we're married to them or not. Take care of yourself. Value yourself. It means you have to pay a little more attention to how and what you're doing, and who you're doing it with. This is what the equation has become. This is what sex looks like today.

Guys will say anything to get laid. They will tell you they love you, they want to be with you, they want to marry you, whatever comes into their horny little heads that they think will seal the deal. But then they come, and they rub their eyes, and they look at you and can't remember your name. What the fuck is that? The girl is left thinking, Wait a minute. You said you wanted to be with me.

Yeah, well I didn't really mean long-term.

Men have a hard time when the situation is reversed. They don't understand why a woman wouldn't want to get involved, or have his kids, or take him into her mouth and swallow him whole. Oral sex is always the great equalizer in a relationship, isn't it? It's a litmus test, and I don't know if guys will ever pass. The fastest way to lose a relationship is to ask a guy to go down on you. That's when you'll know. If he won't, find someone else. If he will, then maybe life will be good. Even if he sucks at it, you can at least teach him. He can learn. Most guys don't like to eat the fuzzy, and the few who do are usually too aggressive or haphazard to make it worth their trouble. They'll chomp at you like cows in a field, you know.

Women used to be sent away to school to learn how to sexually please a man, but these places should be coed, and there should be classes on dick sucking and rug munching *and* everything else too. Why the fuck not? Why do guys ask for head but they're not willing to give it back? Why should it be okay for a guy to get his ya-yas out and go from person to person to person, while if a woman sleeps around she's some kind of slut? This last, I think, is a cultural thing, and it's primarily American. The French don't have that problem. Maybe the English have the same problem, but I don't think the English fuck, so we'll never know. American men don't want their women to have had a whole lot of sexual experience. They want to take you down that road on their Harley. It's okay for them to have been there, because now they know the way, but they want to show it to you for the first time.

Look how long it took women to figure out that they could have an orgasm. Well, yeah. We have these micro-peni. Ultimately, we're packing the same equipment; we just have to search for it and fool with it, but it's ours and it works, same as yours. And who the fuck are you to tell us how much mileage we should have on our equipment? Or how to use it? Or how often? Women are taught we're supposed to give it up to one man, or at least to one man at a time. The man can be out there planting his seed all over the damn place, and the woman is supposed to sit at home and wait for him to pay her some attention. It's such bullshit, and the more we recognize it's bullshit the more we fuck with the balance in male-female relationships. It's a seesaw, and I don't know that it'll ever be level.

We're getting there, though. We're getting to where women now have the strength that comes from experience, from knowing that the world is theirs for the taking. In the old way, it was like watching a *Star Trek* episode, and the woman's trying to beam onto the ship, but her body appears and then it disappears because it's not established yet. Well now we're established and we've beamed onto your ship and you're gonna have to deal with us on our terms. You're gonna have to learn how to give head and get us off and cut us into your double standard because we count as much as you.

NEED

I'M A LIBERAL. I hate the way we've allowed the ideal to get all twisted up and laced with negative connotations, but I don't understand any other point of view. Nothing else washes for me. I'll listen to you, check out what you have to say, but I'll keep coming back to what I think is right, to what I know.

I look at what's happening to our economy, at the jobs we're sending overseas, at the way the haves and the have-nots no longer recognize each other, and I cringe. Here's what I know: Folks at the bottom rungs are having a tough time pulling themselves up to a better place, and folks up top aren't always reaching down to lend a helping hand. I know that I've been at both ends of the ladder, and there's responsibility to be laid on both sides. If you're gonna eliminate a couple jobs because it's cheaper to sub the work out to another plant, or to another country where labor is cheaper, or if you're looking to shift to a part-time work force to avoid paying health and pension and worker's compensation benefits, then I think you have a responsibility to retrain the people you're letting go. You have to set up ways for these people to find other employment. It's not like you're firing them because they're doing a bad job. In fact, you're firing them because they've done a great job, and made you piles of money, and left you in a position to think about making even bigger piles of money. So taking care of these people is the right and moral thing to do.

It's not like IBM or AT&T or Occidental Petroleum ever says, "Hey, guys, over the next five or six years we're gonna scale down a bit and trim a few thousand jobs, but it'll mostly be through attrition and there's probably no need for most of you to worry, and for those of you who should probably worry, we'll give you tons of notice and all kinds of help finding another situation, and a little extra besides." No one ever says that. It's six weeks and you're out. There's no warning. Boom!—you're gone.

It shouldn't go this way. Big businesses get big tax breaks from the government, and the big businessmen still make more money than we have zeroes to account for, but if they're going to take advantage of some of these tax write-offs and incentives they have to put something back. Take care of these people for a while, until they can get their shit together. Why should taxpayers have to dip into their own pockets to subsidize the people you just dumped? It's not right. It's not fair. You let them go. Now you keep them off the streets.

I believe it's the government's responsibility to sit on the neck of Big Business and say, "Hey, motherfucker, if you're gonna have all this work shipped out to some other place because you don't want to have to look after somebody's health benefits, or you don't want to pay the minimum wage, then you can't get these breaks from us." As it is, there just isn't enough relief to go around, and the have-nots are getting the shit end of the stick.

Everywhere we look, we're bombarded with the image of the young (usually black) woman with her thirty-nine kids, talking into the television news microphone, saying, "Well, I'm just laying up, having kids, cashing my welfare checks, doing fine." It pisses me off, big time, as though that's what welfare looks like in this country. Yeah, okay, so that's a part of it, but it's not even close to reality. It's the headline, but it's not the story. Most folks on welfare would love to live decently, to feed, house, and educate their kids in a good environment. The message is that there's work out there, when the truth is that there's not. People, for the most part, want to work. A couple months ago, in New York, there was a job call at a new hotel and thirty thousand people showed up. Thirty thousand! Don't tell me people don't want to work. That should have been a huge story, but it was on at the end of the local news. It didn't even make some of the newspapers in town.

I'm sorry, but you just can't mess with the welfare system without stopping to think how folks wind up there in the first place. You just can't. You can't tell me there are more people on welfare than ever before and think that the way to deal with this is to cut back on programs, or keep people from their entitlements. Yeah, there are more people on welfare, but they're not all black single mothers. They're not all deadbeats and drug addicts and alcoholics living off the system. A great many are working-class folks whose jobs went south, or disappeared with the times and the technology, and they don't want to be on welfare the same as you don't want to be on welfare. They just need some relief for a while, and there's nothing wrong with their looking for it in a system that was meant to serve as a kind of safety net, to look after people. That's why it's here.

It isn't strange, in these times, that people are slowly losing their minds. They're losing their jobs and there's no place to go. They're scared. There is nothing out there for these people, and the more they look the more they despair. Every second, the space between hope and no hope is widening. This could be you. This could be me.

Actually, it was me, for a time. I lived on welfare, as a young mother out in California, and there was no shame in it for me. I'm actually proud of what I was able to do for me and my kid, and I'm not fool enough to think I could have done it on my own. I worked my ass off, trying to keep up, maybe even to save a little to get ahead. I worked with my hands. I held minimum-wage jobs. I did what I could, and what I couldn't do I let the government subsidize. Why not? I earned the right to a cushion—not to rest my butt on, but to break the fall before I hit bottom.

I didn't come to the welfare system without first putting into it. I had all kinds of jobs as a kid. They had the CETA program. They put me to work for very little money, but at least I was working, and no matter how little I was making they took a little something out of my check. I paid my taxes, and I did so thinking the money would be working for me, for when I needed it. I didn't mind that it went to defend the country, or to pave roads I'd never travel, or wherever the hell it went. I didn't mind that we had forty-eight thousand bombs and that I personally didn't think we needed any more, because there were people in charge who apparently thought we did. Great. That was for them to decide. But the money was also there for me, if I needed it, and it wasn't long before I did.

When I was a young mom, I left New York for Lubbock, Texas, to join a friend of mine and work as a nanny to his one-year-old kid. It seemed like a good fit. Our kids were the same age, and I liked taking care of children. I was good at it, and it was good for my little girl to have this built-in playmate. It was almost like having a sibling, which at that point in my life I knew she was never likely to have. It went well at first, and when my friend moved out to San Diego I took my daughter and moved out with him. What the hell did I care where we were? Texas, California, it didn't matter to me. It was a good situation, and I wanted to keep it going, but like most good things it eventually soured, and I found myself in a strange new place with no money to get back home. I couldn't even drive, and if you can't drive in California you're fucked. Shit, even if I could drive I didn't have the money for a car, and I had no skills except for some after-school program stuff I could do with kids, so I was screwed coming and going and staying. I had no high school diploma. I had me, and my kid.

And so I turned to my last, best hope, and started collecting the welfare money I was entitled to, the money I'd paid taxes for. I took the money and kept looking for a job. I talked to lots of people, and was willing to try anything. One guy taught me to lay brick, and I worked with him for a little while, even though you can't make a whole lot of money laying brick unless you're in the union. But this was a good guy, and he gave me as much work as he could, and I was out there laying bricks and cement and doing all this masonry shit, with my little girl at my side. She came with me every day. She's got her handprints somewhere at the San Diego Zoo. Me, I get famous and leave my prints in the cement outside Grauman's Chinese Theatre, and she gets the San Diego Zoo.

After that I met some folks who needed a hair model for their cosmetology school, and all I had to do was sit back and let them do stuff to my hair. Simple enough, right? But let me tell you, it was pretty boring, just sitting there like that, and I started to think it'd be interesting to be the one doing stuff to the hair, to be the hairer instead of the hairee, and the folks running the place were kind enough to give me a scholarship. It was the Deloux School of Cosmetology, and Mr. Deloux was another good soul. If you had an interest, and he found out about it, he let you in. It was kinda great, you know, because I didn't really have any marketable skills or predictable opportunities and I was stuck out there in San Diego, and I couldn't afford the tuition. I was always offering to clean up, or fix things, or do whatever I could to help out around the place and work off the tuition, but they never called on me to do anything except go to the school. It wasn't a loan; they didn't want their money back; they just wanted me to learn. How cool was that?

You had to do sixteen hundred hours before you got your cosmetology degree, and they taught you hair care, skin care, nail care, foot care. It was the whole beauty school package, the works. I was gonna be a cosmetologist. I loved the word. These were the days of the Farrah Fawcett cut, and the Dorothy Hamill wedge. Women with two strands of hair came in wanting to look like Charlie's Angels, and there wasn't much you could do with these two strands but you did your best. You learned that henna could thicken those two strands and leave them looking like six. You learned that if you mixed hair chemicals together you'd better know what you were doing, else you might send the lady who wanted a perm out with a bald head. You learned what the skin could stand, how to treat fingernail fungus and scalp problems. It was a pretty thorough program.

For a while there I cut hair, to earn some extra money, and I got to be a fairly decent stylist, but then I went to work doing hair for a funeral home, working on dead people. It sounds fucked, but it was actually one of the all-time okay jobs. The money was good; you made your own hours; you were left to yourself, pretty much; and the customer rarely talked back. I did makeup, hair, the whole thing, and it was nice and quiet and I could take my kid with me and she wouldn't make too much trouble.

The guy I went out to San Diego with was a theater person, and through him I started hanging out with all these other theater people, and after a while I started trying to get them to hire me—to act, to do hair or makeup—for whatever production they were working on. If you got the gig, the San Diego Repertory Company paid like twenty-five dollars per week, which was scale according to the National Endowment for the Arts.

I did the hair thing during the day, and the theater thing at night, and all the time I was still getting my welfare check. That's what they wanted me to do, get out there and work. It was part of the program. I had to fill out a form every month, detailing my earnings, so I'd put down my twenty-five dollars, or however much I made, and it would be deducted from the welfare check the following month. The accounting system was kinda tough, because if you made less money the second month, your benefits were still cut to reflect what you'd earned the month before; they reduced your benefits by what they expected you to earn. My welfare check was a supplement, but the way they had it set up I didn't feel I could be totally up-front with the government. They actually penalized you, some months, for having worked the month before, so I stopped telling them everything I was doing. The work was sporadic, but the idea of the system was to help me get on my feet and not to screw me up on a technicality. Hey, when you're a single mom, doing what you can to put a reasonable meal on the table, an extra twenty-five or fifty bucks goes a long way.

We lived in a nice house, my daughter and me, in a canyon, in the trees. It was out of a storybook, this place. We were literally on top of the trees, with two giant trunks growing up through the deck, like the fucking Swiss Family Goldberg. There was a bedroom, a living room, and a kitchen, all for $77 per month. Not bad. It was the first house I ever lived in, and I used to sit out on my deck at the end of a tough day and look out over the canyon and think what the future might hold. Shit, the present wasn't all that bad, either. I had my $320 per month from the government, including food stamps, and it stretched far enough to keep us fed and clothed and sheltered and occasionally entertained. It was because of this money that I even had a future to look forward to. Without it, who knows where we would have been?

Years later, when I hit it big, I thought about going back to San Diego to buy our little tree house, and the five or six other houses in the canyon surrounding it. It would be my little string of pearls, a souvenir of a time when things weren't great but good enough. I bailed on the idea, because I wanted the house to stand as I remembered it—not as some real estate holding. It really was a special place. Man, it had a great smell, and it was all green outside, all around, and it was like me and my kid were on top of the world and in the middle of everything, all at the same time. We had a place of our own. We paid the rent. We lived with some dignity, and grace. We mattered.

That's the key, I think, to reinventing our welfare system. We've got to fix it so people can matter—in their own way, in their own communities, in their own families. You could do a pilot program in New York or Los Angeles or any of our big cities, and start asking the folks applying for welfare what kinds of skills they have. You'll find construction workers, nursery-school teachers, bus drivers, people who can work with their hands, all kinds of skills we can put to use. Yeah, there'll be people with no skills at all, but why not start a skill pile, you know? Take all the applicants with something to contribute and start a pilot program and put 'em to work. Put a bunch of people in with a big construction company that gets a lot of city contracts, and get them trained and on the job. Get a day-care thing happening with your teacher pool. Get your plumbers and electricians and rehab some of those abandoned buildings and get them fixed up and running as shelters or community centers. Blow out those crack houses and make real living spaces for real people.

All of a sudden, hey, your welfare check becomes a WPA check, but the money's the same and the community is enriched and people can walk around with their heads up. You've still got your entitlements, but the folks on welfare will be out there working, getting training, putting their skills to use, and if you're able-bodied and don't put yourself up for the work or the training, then you get your benefits cut. You set up a way to deal with the problems people come up with, and you rework the system.

Can a program like this work in a big way? I think so. It's viable, even in some of our more rural areas. It's ambitious, but we can start small, and grow it as you get up to speed. Take fifty people, or one hundred, and see what happens. There are businesses all over the country that can afford to give up a little bit of their materials, or send someone out to supervise job training. All of us haves should start thinking about putting something back.

I want to see the space between rich and poor narrowed in my time on this planet. Okay, I don't mind having to pay for the bomber if you think we need it, but I want you to do some of the things I want done in this country as well. I don't want to hear that kids aren't getting hot lunches because the program's been cut. I don't want to hear that people are getting sick and can't afford medical treatment. I pay a lot of money in taxes, and I'm happy to keep paying it if it can do some good. Shit, I'll pay more, if it'll make any kind of difference. I don't get that we keep funneling all this money into the Star Wars program, or into NASA. You know, I'm sure it's important to figure out if there's life on other planets and whether we can survive in space, but now that we know there is and we can, let's get back to basics. Let's take care of business down here. Let's shave a little money from the budget and try something a little different, see where it goes. You never know.

Everything's all sort of tied into everything else. It's all one ride. Is it a good ride? Yeah, it's okay. It's not bad. It's not an optimum ride, it's not an "E" ride at Disneyland, but if you've been in other countries you know the ride here is not bad. We're not Rwanda, but life could be better for lots of people, and it's within our power to make it so. All we have to do is figure a few things out. Maybe I'll call Michael Eisner and see if there isn't room on the Disney payroll to grab three hundred people from the New York City welfare rolls and put them to work cleaning up Times Square. The Disney theme parks are so completely fucking spotless that I'm sure the city would benefit, and Eisner and company would benefit because they've opened up a new theater there, and a company store, and there's another theater in the works; they'll have the place looking better and they'll generate all kinds of goodwill as a kind of side benefit. We can build good, strong ties with other corporations in other communities, wherever it makes sense, and develop programs that benefit all around. All Michael Eisner and his fellow CEOs can do is say no, but why the hell would they say no? If you can show how the human benefit sets up alongside the various benefits to their company, it'd be hard to look away.

And finally, you can't talk about welfare without looking at immigration. In California especially, there's a lot of noise about illegal aliens crossing our borders and finding work off the books. They're coming because there are jobs. Someone is paying them. Somebody is reaching under the table to give them the $2.12 a week to come and work. To hold the Mexicans or Jamaicans or Guatemalans accountable for wanting to come to America to find work is ridiculous. It's the American employer who's accountable. If I came to you and offered you a job for $2.12 a week, no medical, no cap on hours, you'd tell me to kiss your ass. But there's someone, from some impoverished place, thinking he can make things work on $2.12 a week, and he'll take the job. He will. Everyone has their need, and their price, and it only takes a handful of cheap operators to throw off the whole equation.

Face it: You can't mumble about the goddamn immigrants coming in and stealing our jobs without also wondering what the hell they're doing here. They're working, that's what they're doing, and they're working 'cause we keep giving them work. *We* do this. Not them. Not the government. This one's on us. We have to look at each other and say, "Wait a minute, you have to pay a working wage, you have to pay for health benefits, you have to provide decent working conditions, because that's how we do it here." If our impulse is to get away with whatever we can, we've got to watchdog each other to keep things in check; we have to hold each other accountable.

Yeah, if you give up your workers who work for nothing it means you give up some of your profit. So the fuck what? You'll still make money, just maybe a little bit less. If you give up your maid, you might have to clean your house yourself, or pay what the job deserves. Who's gonna clean your houses, cook your meals, take care of your kids, wash your clothes for $2.12 a week? Tell me. Are we willing to give up our gardeners, and mow our own lawns, and clean our own fucking toilets? That's what should happen if you won't pay a minimum wage. That's the bottom line of it. The responsibility is not with the people who come in and underbid our hired hands; it's not the pickers and the gardeners and the carpenters and the toilet cleaners. They're underbidding us because we've gotten to where we're not going to do those kinds of jobs anymore, and because employers are determined to find the cheapest labor possible. It's human nature. It's the American way. And it sucks.

And yet we're putting out all this information on how it's the Mexican migrant workers taking jobs from the California fruit pickers? It's bullshit. It's like the propaganda the Germans put out about the Jews in the 1930s. It's them. It's their fault that you're not working. If we get rid of them, everything will be better. It's their fault that the black kid and the Asian kid and the Puerto Rican kid grabbed your kid's spot in college. Well, fuck that. We're stuck in this bullshit circle that's spinning us into the twenty-first fucking century, and we don't look at these issues as individual issues. It starts with us, and it ends with us, but we deal with it in big-picture terms. It's a giant whitewash, and we all absolve each other of blame and point the finger to Washington, but it's on us. It's absolutely on us.

HEIR

I'VE HEARD MY MOTHER come out of my mouth more often than I ever could have imagined. It wasn't supposed to be that way. I was gonna do it different. I was gonna reason with my kid. I was gonna be down there with her, and know what it was like, and everything would be cool.

Well, please. Kids just don't give a shit. They want what they want when they want it. Period. They don't want to hear your reasoning. They don't want your solidarity. They'll wear you out, just like you wore out your own parents. There you'll be, hair on end, teeth clenched, quaking with parental indignation, when suddenly you release a phrase or a gesture from too long ago: "I'm the parent, and you're the child." "Because I say so." Something. You'll shake your finger or throw your hands on your hips, same as your mother did, and suddenly you're looking at your own face, and thinking, Oh, shit. Look what I've become—a fax of my folks. An echo.

Grow yourself a teenager and she can go out and pierce every piece of flesh on her body—her cheeks, her eyebrows, her nose, her nipples, her clitoris, everything but her fucking *ears*—and stare back at you like she's daring you to say something about it. And when this happens—and it *will* happen—you'll want to say something, but you know you can't because she won't hear a word. So you wait. You figure, Okay, this girl knows not to put her hand over an open flame. She knows this not because you told her, which you did, but because she checked it out for herself, which she did. She knows because she knows, and eventually she'll know she has to stop putting all these holes in her body, because it just isn't all that comfortable. It just isn't. You'll know the only way to have peace in your house is to be patient. Wait it out and she'll come to the fact that her clitoris hurts, and that she can't rest her head on a pillow with fourteen studs in her face, and that it's a bitch to even blink. She'll come to these things on her own. She doesn't need you.

She'll wake up one morning and look in the mirror and catch that tattoo you told her not to get and think, Damn, why do I have this tattoo of a vomiting devil on my ass? Why didn't I listen to my mother? Because now, if she wants to get that vomiting devil off her ass she's gonna have to go through surgery, and it's gonna cost money and hurt like hell. She'll see that piece of metal in her tongue and go, What the fuck was I thinking? Food will start to taste funny, and she'll know why. She's not stupid; she's just, you know, sorting things through in her own way.

Parents are in a corner. We can't say shit. We're up against hormones; we're up against peer groups; we're up against a sense of fashion we will never understand; we're up against movies and television; and we're up against Alanis Morissette. Our kids are gonna do whatever the fuck they want. They're certainly not gonna listen to us, or take us at our word. They're gonna check it out for themselves. They have to. It's innate to their species.

Kids know better. They know more. And you have to be sort of flexible with that. You have to let 'em move about in their delusions, you know, and hope they realize for themselves that maybe they're a little behind you on this or that, maybe they could use some input. I eventually learned, way after my daughter was an adult, that you can't *always* be patient and wait for kids to come to something by themselves. You can't only be a friend. You must be a parent. Sometimes, you have to let them see you as the bad guy. There is no getting around it.

Prepare yourself: When kids hit that teen tunnel and those hormones start, you are fucked. You can be the best person in the world, the most patient, loving, caring, hippest, smartest, funniest . . . it ain't enough. You are still fucked. You'll never get how they feel or who they are, because you just won't. They don't care how cool you are, or how cool you think you are. You are just not them. They know everything just like you knew everything, and you know nothing just like your parents knew nothing. They sit in their rooms, listening to their music, and you walk in and say, "What the hell are you listening to? I don't like this music. Where's the melody?

What does it mean? What happened to the Supremes?" By the time you start to do the Boston Monkey, you realize what's happening. It's the same as when you were a kid.

"What is this rock 'n' roll? What is this Rolling Stones crap? Why are they dressed like that? Ooooh, they are dirty. Their music is too loud, and too graphic. Put on something else. Put on some Ella."

"Ella?"

"Yeah, Ella, or maybe Sinatra."

Yes, in many ways, we become our parents. It's inevitable. You're going on about your business, doing a better job of it than they ever did, paying more attention, and suddenly your mother's voice comes out of your mouth. It doesn't matter what your situation was as a kid. You take the best from your parents, and you take the worst. You take it all. Abused children become abusive parents because that's what they know. We take our parents with us.

So there I was, with my mother coming out of my mouth. Man, is she smart! I didn't always know it as a kid, and if I did, I certainly didn't appreciate it, but oh, she was smart. She came through her own battles, and raised us on her own, working hard, doing her best, and when she said, you know, "Watch out for this pothole," I should have listened. I didn't—who ever does?—so I fell in the damn pothole.

When my kid was heading for her own potholes, I tried the same as my mother. "Stay away from that pothole," I said, but she didn't listen. Why? Because she knew everything and I knew shit, and she was gonna fall in the fucking pothole no matter what I said.

Now she's a mother too, and she's telling her kid to stay away from the pothole, but the kid's probably not gonna listen either. She'll be on her way to her own pothole, and there'll be a whole chorus of voices—the mother, the father, the granny, the uncle, the great-granny—all trying to keep her from checking out these potholes for herself.

Basically, we humans have this thing about making our own decisions and going our own way. We know we're getting good advice from people who care, but we have to go on our own path anyway. We just do. We have to know it firsthand before we take it seriously. But parents—I'm realizing, still!—have to sometimes go beyond advice and give direct orders. We have to risk the wrath of our children and tell them no. Make it plain. Make it count. You can watch them fall into some potholes, but not all. Some of them, you have to lie your ass down on top and keep them from making the same mistakes you did as a kid. It's your job because you know better. You just do.

One night when my kid was maybe thirteen or fourteen, she came downstairs wearing three pieces of cloth. She said she was going out, and it was none of my business where. I looked this child over, this little version of me. The cloth itself was all shiny and nice and fine, but it wasn't covering enough to suit a mother. It wasn't even close. It was probably against the law, in some states, to go out looking like she wanted to go out looking. Okay, in my time I wore a mini so small that all I needed to do was sneeze and you would have known exactly what color my panties were, but here was my barely teenage daughter, looking like a grown woman, dressed like Madonna used to dress. I completely flipped.

Before my mother could come out of my mouth, she was in my ear. I heard her chuckling in the corner, laughing at me over the way our situation had turned. This was parental justice. Her laugh took me back, and pissed me off. "Why are you laughing?" I shot back.

"Because it's funny," she said. "Because it's funny to see you like this now."

Funny? I'm trying to explain to this child that she can't go out looking like this. She can't go out looking like this because you don't know what invitation someone is going to pick up from this.

That line—you don't know what invitation someone is going to pick up from this—was one of my mother's, and I wanted to suck it right back into my face as soon as I'd said it. My mother looked over at me and smiled, and at first I tried not to smile back, but it was too late. I had to smile too. It wasn't one of those let-me-laugh-along-with-you kinda smiles, or one of those gee-ain't-we-funny kinda smiles, but the kind of smile that comes from knowing. I got it. Finally. I understood. It was a smile of recognition, and maybe a little surrender. I reconnected to everything that had passed between us, and I could see what was coming. I wanted to tell my mother how sorry I was for putting her through all those motions, for not recognizing that she had something to offer beyond what I could see. But she knew. She smiled back and she knew.

I turned to my kid and said, "You know what? Go out. Just go."

And she did. She looked at me kinda funny, and suspicious, but she went out like she'd planned. And then she came back, about twenty minutes later. "You know what?" she said. "It's cold out there. I think I'm gonna change, put a little more on."

It happens, but it takes time. I watch now as my daughter goes through it for herself, with her own kids, and I try not to chuckle. She'll hear me coming out of her mouth and she'll look over with one of those knowing smiles and start to laugh, because we all get it, eventually.

CHOICE

OKAY, SO KIDS can set you straight like nothing else. We've established that. But they can also shake your beliefs right down to their foundations.

My fourteen-year-old called me up on the phone one day. I was on location, and she was in Berkeley. I picked up and she said, "Mom, I'm pregnant." Just like that. There's no other way to say it, I guess. Mom, I'm pregnant. I'd just come in from work and she hits me with "Mom, I'm pregnant."

I sucked in the deepest breath I could find, realized she wasn't kidding, and thought it through. It's amazing how the human mind works at moments of crisis. Or maybe it's just amazing to me how mine works, because in the instant between her telling me and my figuring out what the hell to say I raced through a whole inventory of options and scenarios. I thought the thing completely through, up and down and through, and I kept coming back to the same thing: "Oh, shit!" It wasn't that my mind went blank, because "Oh, shit!'' seemed like a valid enough reaction, but there was nothing clear or adult about it. I mean, this was the last thing I expected to hear from my kid. She had all the information she needed to keep herself from getting pregnant. We had talked. She had understood. And yet here she was, pregnant, and all I could muster was ''Oh, shit! Oh, shit! Oh, shit!''

My initial response seemed so obvious I didn't even see the need to give it voice. I didn't think this was one of those times I could leave my daughter to come to her own decision. I didn't think this should be a discussion. This was just something we had to do. She was fourteen. She wasn't equipped to raise a kid. Emotionally, financially, practically . . . she just wasn't equipped. And I didn't want to raise her kid for her. I'd already done that. I wasn't up for it again.

''Mom?'' I heard through the phone. She wasn't finished, apparently. She had more to tell me. ''I want to keep this baby,'' she said, quietly. Not exactly asking me, but telling me. It was so totally not what I was expecting to hear. The first piece was a shock, and this latest was off the fucking Richter scale.

I still hadn't said anything—although I might have actually uttered a few of those ''Oh, shits,'' I can't be sure—and now I didn't dare. I was back in my corner. I realized that if I was out there screaming to preserve a woman's right to an abortion, I was also out there preserving my daughter's right *not* to have an abortion. I had to take my beliefs out for a little test drive, you know, because prochoice means prochoice, right? It means women (and fourteen-year-old girls) have the choice to do whatever the fuck they want, and here it was my daughter's choice to keep this child. Okay, fine. It bumped smack into what my choice would have been for her, but this is what she wanted.

Man, I'm glad this was what she wanted, because I like my grandkid. She's great. She was born on my birthday. Most kids give you a watch or a wallet on your birthday, or a pocketbook or some flowers, but my daughter gave me a living, breathing human being. The kid even looks like me, a little. She also gave me a lesson. She taught me that "prochoice" is not just a phrase. It doesn't just mean it's okay to go ahead and have that abortion; it also means it's okay not to—if you're responsible, if you've got the support system to back it up, if you've thought it through, if you're prepared to work at it. I was at a time in my career when I was getting some attention and making good money, so my kid had all the financial support she needed, but the rest came from her. She stepped up and became a mother, you know. She needed me, but she didn't *really* need me.

What I don't get from all these prolife people is what they're gonna do for those kids whose parents maybe don't have the resources that were available to my daughter. Because they have to do something. That has to be part of the plan. I'm just waiting for them to lay it out for me, because it's one thing to express your beliefs, but you have to back them up. You have to figure some shit out. I'd be prolife right along with you if you could show me loving homes for every child who needs to be adopted, if you could show me how these young mothers are gonna stay in school and take care of themselves while they're pregnant, if you could show me a system of affordable medical treatment and child care. Show me a viable program of sex education, to get these kids thinking through what they're about to do. Show me a way to take care of these little girls, and their little girls, and then maybe I'll see it your way. Because until then, honey, you're just blind.

Yeah, life is precious. Absolutely. All I need is to hold my grandkid in my arms and the argument is made. I've even got another one now, and it's just precious times two. My daughter had a second child when she was about twenty-two, and her two children are just heaven. She's married now, to a great guy, and they're doing just fine. So don't go hollerin' at me that life is precious. I know. But I also know that freedom and responsibility are precious things, and that if we run out of either, we're screwed.

How many times do you have to open the newspaper to get the point? Every week, it seems there's another story about a young mother abandoning her unwanted child in some Dumpster, somewhere. Rich or poor, it doesn't matter. There are even stories of straight-A students who somehow manage to keep the fact of their pregnancies from their parents and teachers. Now, how the hell do you do that? There's a gap, somewhere in there, that allows a mother to completely miss her kid's nine-month pregnancy. Something's missing. And what about gym class, at school? How the hell can they not notice something like that? But it happens all the time, and if it keeps happening it means someone, somewhere is dropping the ball.

So let's get it straight: Prochoice means you can go either way. If you get pregnant, decide what you want to do. Do you want to have this child? Are you able to have this child? Will you be able to finish school, or get a job, or look forward to any kind of productive future? Shit, you should decide on these things *before* you go out and get pregnant, but I realize that's probably asking too much. Just decide at some point, early on. Think it through and decide, and if you decide not to have the child, for whatever reason, you should be able to have a clean, safe abortion, with dignity and respect.

We were lucky in our house, and it worked out, but shit like this ain't supposed to be about luck.

DRIVE

I USED TO THINK of myself as a politically sensitive person. Forget politically correct. Sensitive. The wolf P.C. has no place in comedy, and I don't see where it fits in our culture. Yeah, you don't want to offend people. You don't want to say, "Damn, baby, you have got to be the fattest woman alive. Don't even come in the door because you will break my house down." You don't want to tell someone their voice is grating, or their teeth are yellow, or their taste sucks. You don't want to box people in little stereotypes, and start making assumptions. But you still want to be true to what you believe and what you think is right, because if you do what makes sense to you, what feels right, then you're cool. Your ass is covered. To hell with what everybody else thinks.

Now, let me set this last point aside, because as it turns out I'm not as politically sensitive as I used to think. I'll cop to it, and explain. Put me behind the wheel of a car, and everyone's an asshole. Everyone's a stereotype. Old people. Black people. Asians. Short people. We've all got our little routines. All of us, that is, except me. No one deserves to drive like I deserve to drive. That's my philosophy. No one pays attention like I pay attention. Why the fuck do all you people have licenses, anyway? You, you're too old to be behind the damn wheel. You, you're too crazy. You can't even see out of your windshield, and you cut me off. Where did you get your license, Woolworth's? You know. I'll roll down the window and yell at everybody, and I won't give a shit what comes out of my mouth.

Oh, you do that too? Hmmmm . . . well, the truth is I'm probably just an okay driver. Just okay. I don't like to go way too fast. I don't like to go way too slow. I'm always afraid no one will see me. I used to ride a motorcycle, and no one ever sees you on a motorcycle. So now I use my blinker, I use hand signals, I put up fucking neon signs. I don't sneak up on people, or surprise the folks behind. But when I'm driving, I'm the diva of the road. Don't even think about fucking with me when I'm driving.

But when it comes to everyone else, nothing is sacred . . .

Black people pay no attention in the car. None. They talk, they sing, they gab with their friends, they take in the scenery. Then, if something happens, they will get out and wail on you. I don't know anyone else who does this, except maybe cabdrivers, but black people will get out of their cars and scream at you for their fuck-up.

Not me, though. I turn the music up until my ears are bleeding and I bounce along, singing the songs, not going too fast, not going too slow, and once in a while I guess I stop a little short, or I signal too soon, and the people behind me are cursing me out. They peg me as just another crazy black driver, but I don't get out of the car and scream. Okay, I roll down the window and scream, but I don't get out. What's the point of getting out? And I'm not crazy. I'm completely fucking sane. I've just got my music cranked loud so I don't have to listen to yours.

And there's a reason people make jokes about Asian people in the car. It's because they can't drive for shit. Not all Asian people, mind you—just the ones fool enough to share the road with me. You know who you are. Now, I'm sure there are many Asians with spotless driving records, and maybe even a few who've never been given the finger, but I haven't seen them. The ones I've seen are all over the road, flitting in and out of lanes, turning without signaling, driving as if they owned the damn road. Okay, so these might be *your* cars, but you're driving on *my* road.

Old people? They drive like they're just remembering what they're supposed to do. They're going along, and they're going along, slowly, and it suddenly hits them that they *must* go left. Immediately. And then they just go to the left. They don't look. They don't signal. Boom. They just go. They make all these sudden left turns from the far right lane, and then they're always surprised when they hit something. And you can't really yell at them because they're too old. Even I know not to do that. But I want to say, "Look, you know, take the bus. Here's a token. Take the motherfucking bus."

Then you've got your low drivers. You've seen these people. They've got the seat down low, and you look over and you can maybe see the tops of their heads. It's cute, in an annoying sort of way. You can see one eye. Their arms are stretched and raised above their heads, and they're doing ninety. They're weaving in and out and cutting you off and you can't even see them. Okay, so maybe they're short, but my feeling on this one is if you're short, sit on a fucking phone book. Get a pillow. Pull the seat up close. Something. Find some way to get your head above that steering wheel and let other people see you because it just freaks us out to look over and see these cars driving themselves. That's what it looks like, sometimes, like a fucking George Romero movie gone berserk. There's no one at the wheel, and we've got no idea what you're gonna do.

Now, New Jersey drivers have a tough time in the car. I don't know what it is, but if their plates say Jersey, they are going to fuck with you on the road. Expect it. They are going to sit their big-ass American sedans in front of you in traffic, and lean on their big-ass American horns, and never let you in their lane. And if you ride them about being from Jersey they'll flip you the bird.

People in Los Angeles get a bad rap. The driving is crazy-making, but the drivers aren't always insane. There's an orderliness to the mess of driving in L.A. that you don't get in a city like New York. Maybe the threat of drive-bys and car-jackings has scared people into toeing the line a little bit, but L.A. drivers are actually somewhat predictable. You can kinda guess their moves. New York drivers, I've got no fucking clue, but then most people in Manhattan don't drive, so you're dealing mostly with cabdrivers and people from Jersey.

What I won't do in the car is put on makeup, or eat, or do my hair, or make like I can't be bothered with driving. If you catch me doing any of these things, just pull me over and yell. What's the deal with these people? They're on the phone, they're typing shit on their laptops, they're cookin' breakfast. It's like they're too busy to get where they have to go. I was on the New Jersey Turnpike once, coming back to New York from Atlantic City, and there was a guy reading the fucking newspaper while he was driving. I've seen people read at stoplights, or in bumper-to-bumper traffic, but this asshole (with the Jersey plates!) was doing seventy and reading the paper.

It's amazing to me what people do. They don't realize, you know, that being in the car is being in the car. You have to look at what you're doing, pay attention, think. You have to drive. That's it. If you're driving, and you've got one of those hands-free phones, and you've got to take a call, then take the call and don't make a big thing out of it. But don't go looking through your phone book for a number, or rifling through your papers, or sending a fax, or checking the latest stock quotes. That's not acceptable.

People have no clue that you can see them when they're in their cars. It's a funny thing. They shut the door and turn the key and it's like they're in their own little world. They've got their stereo, they've got their phone, they've got their computer, and their little drink holders, and maybe an extra makeup kit in the glove compartment. It's like an apartment on wheels, and no one can see in.

And if you're in a low car, you can just forget about it. The people in high cars can see down and in. They can see everything. One time, on the Long Island Expressway, coming back from Astoria Studios, I looked down from an elevated truck and saw a guy getting a blow job. He's getting a blow job and I'm thinking, Well, this is kind of fun. He's just driving along with this woman's head in his lap, getting his rocks off, not giving a shit, because the car, for him, is just an extension of his home. It's like a branch office.

Women who drive with their tops off, or men with their peckers out, are just amusing, but folks don't know where to stop. People who pick their noses in cars should be arrested. There should be a law. I don't understand this thing about picking your nose in the car. Nothing grosses me out more than anything that comes out of the nose. The stuff makes my skin crawl. I know everybody gets colds and runny noses, but leave me the fuck out of it.

These people digging away in their noses at stoplights are completely offensive. It's an affront to have to look at these assholes prospecting. I'd turn away if I could, but I'm trapped. Everyone's doing it. Turn this way, the guy's picking his nose. Turn that way, there's another guy picking his nose. And they don't stop at picking. They dig, they take it out, they look at it, inspect it, consider it. It's one of the things I think cops should pull people over for. You know, grossing out other drivers. Do it at a red light, the fine should be fifty bucks. Do it driving at high speed, it should be fifty bucks, plus a buck per mile on the speedometer, plus maybe some community service.

We've all gotten a little too weird about our cars and what it's okay to do inside them. You can even buy these portable toilet things, for those long drives and urgent needs, and I suppose this makes sense. It's a natural extension of where we're going. I mean, we hang our clothes up in the back, in case we have to change. Some people carry an extra pair of shoes. We take along our books and newspapers. We put pictures of Jesus Christ, or Tupac, on the dash. Room freshener. Little decorations hanging from the rearview mirror. We even have televisions you can plug into cigarette lighters, which doesn't make much sense to me. But okay, who the fuck am I to judge? I'm just the asshole who signals a couple hundred yards too soon, who sings at the top of her lungs, who knows—at all times—exactly what she's doing, who will never pull up at a red light with her finger up her nose or a Big Mac between her teeth or a cell phone to her ear or a Portosan tucked under her butt or a television tuned to CNN.

Hey, if I'm running late, I'm running late. There's nothing I can do on the fly that will get me where I have to be any faster, or with any dignity.

DEATH

I WAS PRETTY MUCH AN ADULT before anyone I really knew died. It's weird to me now, looking back on how we lived, but death wasn't part of our world. We had Mister Softee, stickball, Coney Island, school dances, the candy store . . . but death wasn't in my frame of reference. I knew what it was, but it didn't touch me, not directly. It was distant and old and for someone else. Grandparents were gone by the time you were born, or they lived forever. Black people lived forever. At least it seemed that way. We got old and wise and we didn't wrinkle, except for Jane Pittman, and she didn't wrinkle until she was about two hundred years old. And really, we didn't check out until some natural cause came to claim us.

But death, now, is in our face. It's everywhere. Little kids live with their mortality every day—at school, walking down the street, on the six o'clock news. It's never out of their minds, and this came slamming home to me with my own daughter. She was about fifteen, and going out to the park with her friends. She was always going to the park with her friends, especially when her child was staying out of town with my mom, only this time she went out for just a half hour or so before she returned. This never happened with my kid. When she went out, she went out. Maybe you saw her a couple hours later, maybe not, but you never saw her in just a half hour.

I asked her what she was doing back so soon.

"There was a drive-by," she said, like it was the most natural thing in the world.

"What do you mean there was a drive-by?" I knew, but I needed to hear it.

"Someone drove by and started shooting. That kind of drive-by."

"Was anyone hurt?" I wanted to know.

"Someone was shot," she said. Calm as anything.

This wasn't shocking to her, that someone was shot. It didn't freak her out. It totally freaked me out, but she was okay with it. It made sense to her. She said, "Ma, it's okay. I'm fine. It happens a lot. Someone gets pissed off at someone else, and they start shooting."

The cool indifference rolled from my daughter like nothing at all. Drive-bys were just something that happened. All the time. And she was okay with it.

Understand, I wasn't blind to what was going on in the streets, but it's one thing to know it on an intellectual level and another to know it firsthand. Kids my daughter's age saw this kind of violence every day, and they were numb to it. It didn't register for them the way it registered for me, because when violence is the norm, death isn't anything. For my daughter, this had just been another day at the park. For me, it was a cruel awakening. She and her friends went upstairs, but I had to go out for a walk. I had to figure this out. I worked to understand what I'd just seen, through the eyes of my child. Whatever it was, it was disturbing as hell. It told me what I suppose I already knew—that she was growing up in a world completely different from the world I knew as a kid. Violence, real violence, was a part of her, in a way that it still wasn't a part of me, in a way that it would probably never be a part of me. I didn't know shit about *present* violence. The violence I knew wasn't present, outside-your-door violence. It was on-television violence, make-believe violence, and if it got too real I could always change channels.

When I was a kid, nobody died on television. If they did, they were the bad guys. Check out those Nick at Night reruns if you don't believe me. Nobody died on *Leave It to Beaver*. Maybe Lumpy had a bad day, but he didn't pull out an AK-47 and blow people away. There were drunks in the lockup in Mayberry, but there were no rapists or serial killers. Even on *Mannix* or *The Mod Squad* or *Mission Impossible,* the violence was always offscreen, or understated. Now people die all the time on television. Every couple minutes, someone's getting whacked. You can see a bad guy hacking up a victim's body into twenty-seven pieces and stuffing it into garbage bags. You actually see the blood and the body parts and everything. On medical shows, people die all the time. There's blood everywhere, every week, leading into every commercial. They showed blood on *M*A*S*H,* but there was a laugh track underneath. This is different.

This is an emergency room where surgeons are up to their elbows in blood and guts, where children, riddled with bullets, are rolled in on gurneys.

It's very different now. In the old days, you made an appointment to fight each other, you set a specific time and place, so no one else would be around. If there was a rumble, you went out and hit each other with your fists. Maybe you used brass knuckles. Once in a while you'd hear about chains, or rocks, or maybe even knives, but the violence was mostly hand-to-hand, and it was never random. There was a code, a sense of right and wrong. People got the shit beat out of them, or they got cut, but they got cut for a reason, and nobody was supposed to die. That was the rule. But now it's gotten to where people can just drive by and kill you and it won't even make the front page. It doesn't dent our consciousness. They shoot and then go about their business as if nothing happened. They don't give it a thought.

Maybe I'm crazy, or old-fashioned, but I kinda liked things the way they were. I'd rather have folks fighting each other away from everyone else, off in a back alley somewhere, if that's what they feel they have to do. Keep the bullshit confined. That way at least the rest of us could walk about in relative safety, but the way things have turned, everybody is at risk. When did this happen? And why? I've got no fucking clue, but it scares the shit out of me. It's got me thinking anything can happen, you know, nothing is certain; you can leave the house in the morning and come back hacked into twenty-seven pieces, stuffed into garbage bags.

Violent death is all over the place now. Death, in general, is all around. It's a bummer, but I find ways to deal, and one of those ways is to develop a bigger picture. I believe we come into this world through a revolving door; we leave and then we come back again. Call it reincarnation or whatever you want to call it, but when I look at children who are ill, or dying, I know that they will come back in some other body, in some different form. I know they'll get another shot at a happy ending; I know they will be at peace. Our spirit survives us just as it precedes us, which is why I think it's important to talk about the people in your life who have died. You have to talk about the fact that they were here, and celebrate what they left behind.

The first person close to me who died was a dancer friend of mine in San Francisco. He died of AIDS before it had a name. This was back in the early eighties. We got Reagan and we got AIDS, and both were pretty frightening. My friend broke out into these big red blotches and had all this white yeast in his mouth, and no one could figure what was wrong—not the doctors, not the media, no one. It was *clear* he was dying, but that was all anyone knew. We didn't know shit. I sat with him thinking, How could something like this happen? Would it happen to me? Was it contagious? Should I bail, to protect myself? But if I bailed, what kind of a friend would that make me? What if my kid got it? What the fuck is it? All we knew was what it wasn't. It wasn't cancer. It wasn't anything in any of the medical texts. It wasn't anything we'd been conditioned to expect. It wasn't like he'd been hit by a bus, which would've at least been something we could understand. It was just this huge, scary void. It was too unreal. My friend had been active, and in great shape. He was young. Shit like this wasn't supposed to happen to somebody young.

But it did, and it does. It happens all the time. Now it happens so often that when a friend dies of something other than AIDS it's almost a relief. I had a great friend called Lester, a wonderful choreographer, and when he died of a heart attack I remember thinking, Wow, what a relief! A heart attack. How quaint. A heart attack I could understand. It was a terrible thing to lose him, but a heart attack made sense. I guess when you lose so many friends to an epidemic, you kinda block yourself off; you don't fall to scattered pieces every time. You get harder each time—so people can depend on you, so you can get through it—and it's only when someone dies for some different, more understandable reason that you get your chance to fall apart.

I actually heard myself telling a friend how cool it was that Lester had gone in this more old-fashioned way, and I realized that AIDS has changed the stakes. Oh, it has. Most of us have been touched by the disease, and we've been left in a completely new way. It's put us more in the moment, taught us to live hard and all out and full speed ahead, and yet at the same time more carefully. And do you know what? Death doesn't knock the wind out of me and send me to the ground the way it once did. Now, when my friends go, I think, Damn, what happened? I weigh the manner of their leaving against how they might have gone and come away thinking how lucky, or how sad, or whatever. It's got me thinking that it matters, how we die, that you can't cheat death but if you can at least cheat this fucking disease then maybe you've done okay.

. . .

I want to go doin' the do. There's no other way. Natural causes, in the arms of someone I care about, without pain or warning, in the middle of some wild fucking. Forget peaceful. I want to go when I'm with someone who is at least interested in the fact that I'm here, and I can just lay back and say, "Ooooh," and be gone. Go out with a bang, right? Well, maybe there's something to it.

I don't want to be shot. I don't want to die because of someone else's screwup. I don't want to die on some operating table because some dumb surgeon wasn't paying attention. I don't want to fall out of the sky in an airplane. I don't think I'm afraid to die, but who needs all that time to think about it, on the way down? I want to go calmly and quickly and with some dignity. A little pleasure, and then I'll see you later.

And I absolutely don't want to stay on past my time. If my time is up, then my time is up. That's why I'm a big fan of Dr. Jack Kevorkian. I hate the way we've dubbed him "Dr. Death," because that's so not what he's about. He's not about death. He's about hope and grace, honor and choice. He's about taking control of how things go. He should have an 800 number, you know, like a hot line. If you know you've got to go, you might as well go out in style. What's the point of staying around until you're in so much pain you could eat the entire hospital? What's the point of running up such a huge medical bill your family will never get out from under it? I want to know that some guy is there that I can call. 1-800-DOC-JACK. I want to know that if I'm sick enough, and if everybody knows I'm sick enough, and if there's no way out but an agonizing, pain-in-the-ass exit, that I can take control of my own body and check out on my own terms. You have to be sick enough. Kevorkian doesn't just go and kill you because you ask him to. He doesn't just come over and say, "Oh, you've had enough?" and that's it. He puts you through a whole number. That's the guy I want.

Have you heard about this 1-800-FUNERAL number they've been advertising on the radio? It's like 1-800-FLOWERS. You can call up and order a mahogany casket, or pine, or ash, and you can have it lined in velvet or silk, or whatever the hell you want. You can do it all with a simple phone call, so it's not a big deal. You can even order the cremation option, if that's the way you want to go. (They've probably got this great *I Dream of Jeannie* urn that looks kinda cool.) It's such an odd aspect of our culture, the way we humans deal with death, that when we're faced with a practical solution to all the mundane details surrounding it we get all strange about it. Why is that? Why shouldn't there be a toll-free number? Why shouldn't a Jack Kevorkian swoop in and set you off with some dignity?

The key, I think, is to die on your own terms. If I can't go fucking, I just want to go quietly, without interruption. It pisses me off when people get in my way now, when I'm healthy, and when the time comes that I'm not I don't want them shooting me full of stuff, and keeping me breathing on those respirators, and floating my brain in a jar, or whatever the fuck they can do to prolong my life without my permission. I don't want no interruptions. They didn't do that in the old days. Back then, if you were on the edge of going, maybe they gave you a little shove. They helped you along. Oh, you're going anyway, we need the bed, please understand. But now you have the doctor for the toenail, and the doctor for the toenail bed, and everybody has all these specialties, and frankly you are no better off, really.

Yeah, you can prolong the inevitable, but that shit's still gonna find you. If your body is giving out, your body is giving out. The Hippocratic oath was fine in its time, because everybody died anyway, but science has caught up to it. Times have changed. Even the Bible has to be amended, you know, so while we're at it let's rewrite the fucking Hippocratic oath. The old doctors did their best and, poof, you were gone, but the new guys pull all kinds of shit and keep you going simply because they can. Not because it makes sense. Not because there's a good chance you'll get back to how you were. But because they can.

Elephant doctors don't take the Hippocratic oath. Wildebeests don't take the Hippocratic oath. Lions and tigers and bears don't know shit about no Hippocratic oath. I'm tellin' you, we could learn a few things from the Discovery Channel. We humans must have missed school the day the rest of the animal kingdom figured it out: The herd is running across the tundra, and one of the beasts pulls up and says, "I don't think I can make it." Well, the rest of the herd just looks back and says, "See ya." They don't even break stride, because if they stay there with him they're going to die. It's eat or be eaten, kill or be killed, mope or move on.

Yup, the elephants have it down. They go off on their own, to die in peace, with their history. They say, "Look, it's been great, see ya later. Gotta go." And they go to the big elephant graveyard and hang around the bones of their ancestors. They just hang there and take it all in and think, This is where I'm going. This is what it all comes to.

There's no human equivalent, but the concept is pretty cool when you break it down. We should just go off and hang with the spirits of our parents or grandparents or brothers or sisters or whoever the hell has gone before us and kind of ease into what's gonna happen. Hey, you know, what's it like, over there, on the other side? How you been? What's up with this? Do you still get cable?

Who do these people think they are, trying to take death out of our hands? It's the last thing we get to do, and we've got some extremist group in Pook-a-Doop, U.S.A., deciding they don't like the way we're living our lives. They don't like that we can choose when to go, and how. Why is this anybody else's business? Why shouldn't we be able to go in whatever way makes us most comfortable? We should be left to live our lives right up till the very end. We should have the right to surround ourselves with people who know what they're doing, like Doc Jack. We should be at home, with the people we love. We should talk about it more, so that when we're ready to go and say good-bye it isn't this horrific thing. We should put it in context. We've been here before. We'll be back again.

WORD

WHO DECIDES WHAT'S OKAY to say in polite conversation, and what's not? Did I miss a meeting? Is there some lofty group of people voting on all these words and phrases? If there is, I'd like to know what the vote was on *fuck*, and who voted, because *fuck* isn't a bad word.

Most people don't even know what *fuck* means, or where it comes from. I'll give you one explanation. In the Puritan days, we dragged adulterers into the streets and put 'em in the stockades and posted a big old sign next to them describing their crime: FOR UNLAWFUL CARNAL KNOWLEDGE. The words were stacked so that the initials—F.U.C.K.—took on their own meaning. That's all it is, fuck, and yet people have attached all kinds of ugliness to it, and hatefulness, and perversion, but it's just a word, man. It's just shorthand for what was once considered a crime.

You have to consider the source. You have to stop and think, Okay, what is it about this word that makes me so uncomfortable?

Why is it pissing me off? Does it make me mad because I think you're an asshole? Does it make me mad because you think *I'm* an asshole? It's our perception of bad words that gets us going, and here I think it's helpful to look at the problem through the eyes of a child. To a three-year-old, *pee-pee lips* is the same as *fucking asshole*. The intent is the same, but some parent always comes along and says, "Don't say this, Junior, because it's bad." Why is it bad? Is *Leave me alone, pee-pee lips* any less clear to the receiver than *Leave me alone, you fucking asshole*? At three years old, they're the same thing.

If you've got a little kid who likes to walk around her classroom saying, "Fuck, fuck, fuck," you have to consider the source. She's a little kid. She doesn't know what the word means. Oh, it means sex? Well, what is sex? When you're three, sex is just another bad word. Fuck, fuck, fuck. Sex, sex, sex. They're just words she likes to say. No buildings fall when she says them. No one drops dead when she says them. I'd be worried if she was walking around saying, "Hate, Hate, Hate." But *pee-pee lips, ca-ca head, shit, fuck, sex, doody bomb, asshole* . . . these are just new, funny-sounding words that little kids for some reason love to say. We can't get mad at 'em for what they don't understand. If we can't handle it, we should come up with new words, some okay words, for our kids to build into their vocabulary. *Leave me alone, you gaggle bottom* is pretty clear, and if parents are more comfortable with nonsense, then I suppose that's cool.

It doesn't matter what some little kid calls you, and it shouldn't matter what a regular-size grown-up person calls you either. We are what we are, and we know what we are. Take the word *nigger*. Now,

I've never been a nigger. Don't really know what a nigger is. That's why I've never been one. Maybe other people have thought I was a nigger, but that's their definition. And yet people hear the word *nigger* and they run from it, or they're stopped by it, or they get an attitude about it. Why? Is it because, deep down, you feel it's true? If that's the case, then why is it okay if a person calls himself a nigger? Does that make it a term of inclusion, and if so what exactly are we including ourselves in?

The word *nigger* wasn't used in a negative way in my youth, growing up in New York. It was out there, and all around. One of Richard Pryor's best albums was even called *That Nigger's Crazy*, so here was a word that appeared on the front of an album cover that said, "Yeah, that's a crazy brother, that's a crazy man." To me, I think, Oh, all right, he's funny. That's cool. Eddie Murphy uses it in his routines, and they're funny. It's not a negative thing. The words are out there. They're not being spoken in the quiet of people's homes. They're out there, and all kinds of people are buying these albums, and they're all laughing, and thinking, Well, okay, niggers are funny. So, some white guy is moved to shout out, Hey, nigger, you funny! And what happens? Gone. Broken noses, car fires, all kinds of shit happens, and it just flows from this one word.

When Jackie Mason talks about a Jew, it's funny, but if I step onstage and start talking about, "Oh, there goes an old Jew," then there's trouble. I become a black person, speaking negatively to describe another person. I cross a line. If a Jewish person uses the word *kike* or *Jew* in telling a story about his own brother, and if this is okay, then why isn't it the same when a non-Jewish person uses the same word to describe the same man? What about a Spanish person, or a lesbian person? Is *spic* or *dyke* any more or less offensive depending on who says it? If it's not malevolent, or mean-spirited, I don't care what the hell you call me, and I reserve the right to call you by whatever name I choose.

So I'm thinking we have to defuse these words, declassify them, so that we can use them for what they are. They're funny words. They're meaningless words. So let's declassify them and put them out on the open market, and strip them of any weight and power, and leave them to be used in light, dopey ways. Like *fuck*. *Fuck* is a word you can use positively or negatively. Why can't we do the same with *nigger, Jew, spic, wop*? If you declassify them, make them the same as *fuck* and *shit* and *asshole,* then they can be used in those same ways. And then no one will ever have to deal with anything but the intent of the user. Once again, just consider the source. Take the secret-handshake element out of them, and leave them as words for everyone to use. *That fucking coat is beautiful. That coat is beautiful.* As opposed to, *That fucking coat is awful. That coat is awful. That nigger's crazy. That man is crazy.*

I was involved in an incident a couple years back. I wrote a bunch of material for someone else to say, which is how it goes sometimes in the entertainment business. You read someone else's words. Someone else reads your words. You know. When you go to see *Rosewood,* and Jon Voight says *nigger*, he's got an attitude when he says it. He says it negatively, because that's the character he's playing, that's the way it was written, but no one goes out and strings up

Jon Voight because of it. We get that he's just reading his lines, that he's just acting. We don't hold him to it.

But the people held me to mine. Man, did they string me up and hold me to it, and I still don't get why. The material I wrote was funny, 'cause I tend to write funny stuff, 'cause I'm a funny person. And the person who was reading my lines, who happened to be white, performed the material as I wrote it. He was a white man, made up in black face, performing material written for the occasion by a black woman. It was no different than if I had gotten up on that platform and said the words myself. It was a piece written about me, by me, that I put into the mouth of a character.

And that should've been where it ended. We should've had a few laughs, and gone home. But that's not where it ended. There was a whole big stink. People still talk about the stink we made. It won't go away. Richard Pryor could have delivered the same material on himself and people would have been pissing themselves in the aisles, they would've been rolling, and then they would've gone home and moved on. But when I got a white man to dress up like a black man, playing a character that I wrote for him, to say these things on me, folks were outraged. I put these words in his mouth, and these were words that everyone would have been okay with if they'd come out of Chris Rock's mouth, or Eddie Murphy's mouth, but for some reason they were off limits to me and my character. Now, people will generally take it from a guy much faster than they will from a woman. I kinda understand that. And people expect you to respect these polite boundaries we set up for ourselves for what's okay. I understand that, too. I don't stand up in church and start talking nasty, even if it's just the funny and frivolous kind of nasty, because there's a time and a place for everything, right? But these lines weren't delivered in church. This performance wasn't at the Junior League. This was a performance for other twisted sisters and funny people like myself. This was an inside, entertainment-industry gathering, where other people have said far more outrageous things, from time to time, dressed in far more offensive garb, but these lines just made a whole big stink. And it got me wondering what it is we're fighting against. Prejudice, that's one thing, but these words, to me, don't embody prejudice. Actions embody prejudice, because there are people who will come and pat you on the head and tell you how much they love you, and truly hate you, and they'll never use a word like *nigger*. So we have to deny these words their power. We have to make the discussion about the intent, and not the language.

For a time there, television censors were the arbiters of what was okay to say and what was not okay to say. If you couldn't say it on television, you couldn't say it at the dinner table. But now you hear people say all kinds of shit on television. You hear it on cable, over the airwaves, all over the fucking place. I heard Roseanne say *asshole* on network television. It shocked the shit out of me. You can say *damn*. You can use words that resemble other words: *bleep you, no effing way*. You still can't take God's name in vain, but we're getting there. I sit at home and see how we're moving to a more enlightened place and think, Okay, here we are. Finally. Christ, it's about fucking time.

Sometimes it's not just a word that gets people in trouble, but a whole way of thinking. We haven't reached the place yet where it's okay to put your foot in your mouth on a public stage, or show yourself as you truly are. If you use some racial slur, or reveal some racist thinking, you're screwed. Remember Jimmy the Greek? He opened his mouth and said that the big black bucks mate with the big black women and make really fast kids. He didn't know any better. He was a nice, simple man who meant to say blacks tend to be faster than whites, and he was run out of town for it. Just run out of town. Nobody said to him, "Jimmy, you might want to find a different way to phrase that, because we don't like being called big black bucks anymore." And do you know what? We've got a lot of big white bucks playing football. And Samoans. And all kinds of people. But they fired his ass and sent him away, and what the hell does that say about the rest of us? We all make mistakes. Sometimes we need to let those mistakes slide, you know. Sometimes we need to be bigger than the folks who don't know any better. I'm not saying we should tolerate ignorance, but maybe we should be a little more tolerant of ignorant people who step in shit and need to learn from it, or want to learn from it.

The same thing happened to Al Campanis, the guy from the Los Angeles Dodgers, who told Ted Koppel on *Nightline* that black people were less buoyant than white people, which explained why there weren't any world-class black swimmers. I mean, come on! He also said that most blacks didn't have the "tools" needed to manage a major league baseball team. I don't know, it seems to me our boys can chew tobacco and spit and scratch themselves and sit on their asses with big beer bellies hanging over their belts about as well as any white person. Ol' Al was run out of the Dodgers' front office before the poor sap even realized what he'd said, and black folks were calling for his head, but no one stopped to consider that the man just didn't know any better. Neither Al Campanis nor Jimmy the Greek actually said the word *nigger,* so you see it isn't just the word but the intent that grips the gut.

Tex Antoine was a local weatherman on WABC-TV in New York when I was a kid, and he didn't limit his ignorance to one race of people. He listened to Roger Grimsby, the anchorman, read a really horrendous story about a woman who was raped, and then said that if she had simply sat back and enjoyed it she'd have probably been fine. He said this on live television. They didn't even wait for the man to do the weather. They cut right to commercial and removed his ass from the set, and he showed up a few years later on one of the smaller, independent channels in town, but he never got his career back. He was one of the biggest stars on the local television news scene, and he was done, but when you think about it, what did middle-aged men know about rape? We're still trying to get people to understand it. People just don't know, and you can't kill them for not knowing. If they don't learn from their mistakes and show the same stripes all over again, then you can kill them. But you can't kill them the first time out.

And then there's a cat like Jesse Jackson. Here's a guy who wasn't a sports commentator, or a weatherman. He didn't have a weekly show. But he came out and called New York "Hymie-town" and people were ready to light him on fire, because after all, this was a guy who was supposed to be part of the Rainbow Coalition, uniting all these different groups. He had this great lapse, with a microphone on him, and he just forgot that there were all kinds of people in New York and made a stupid statement. And there's no way to clean up a statement like that. Even if they had brought Tex Antoine back, what would he have said? You know. How could Jimmy the Greek make you understand that what he meant to say was . . . ? So you do have to consider the source. There is no comeback to some of this shit.

So now Jesse Jackson doesn't run for president anymore—or, if he threatens to, nobody seems to care. He wasn't working for a television station, so there was no one to fire him, but we stopped taking him seriously. Jesse Jackson's punishment was that the people who believed in him no longer do. He's got some talk show, somewhere, and he turns up on the news and makes his speeches, and we listen with a quarter of an ear.

If we think about forgiving people their trespasses, as we forgive those who trespass against us, then we have to be bigger, regardless of what these words seem to mean. In reality, *big black bucks* should have meant nothing. *Hymie-town* should not have been an insult, because there is no Hymie-town. Maybe there's Hymie Smith, you know, but there's no Hymie-town. And women should not lay back and enjoy it, and Tex Antoine should have known better, but we have to give some thought to these things. Even in the case of Marge Schott, probably the biggest foot-in-mouth in the United States of America, we must consider the source. People have the power we give them. Words have the power we give them. And if we can declassify these words, we'll have a much easier time of it, and people will then become responsible for what they say—not for the way it affects me, but for what they say.

Consider the source. That's what it comes down to. Say whatever the fuck you want. Call me whatever the fuck you want. What counts is how you say it, and how you live your life, and whether or not you're willing to change.

DICK

SAY . . . WHY IS IT that most things in the world are shaped like a man's penis? Am I the only one who notices this? Pencils, lipstick, 747s, vacuum-cleaner nozzles, baseball bats, the Empire State Building. Coke bottles? Bottles, for the most part, are all shaped like penises. They even name things after parts of the penis. There's a car called the Corona, a beer called Corona, a cigar called Corona, a tip of the penis called corona.

Now, women don't obsess about their vaginas the way men do about their penises. We just don't. We don't build these vagina-shaped tributes to ourselves. You'll notice there are no cars called Vagina or Vulva. There's a Volvo, but there is no Vulva. We don't worry about the size of our clitoris. We don't think about the width and the depth of it.

So what is it about the penis? Is there some kind of club that little boys go to? Some pledge you all make, or some mysterious initiation you go through? Are there magic powers associated with your divine rods? Maybe there's a course you all take, but if there is, believe me, you're not getting all the necessary material, because you guys are at a loss when it comes to going to the bathroom. I'm sorry, but who taught you how to shake? Not to wipe, mind you, but to shake? Most men I know say they learned by watching what other guys were doing, so I visualize this line of little boys sort of looking over to see how it works, side to side and up and down, but not wanting to be seen. But what if nothing's happening on one of these trial runs? What if there's a whole line of little boys, none of them knowing what to do? Is there some unspoken rule that you don't ask for directions? Do you just decide it's okay to do your business and zip your things back into your pants while they're still wet?

I don't have pet peeves, like some people. I've got whole kennels of irritation, and the wet spot on men's pants when they leave the john is just beyond my understanding. I don't get it. Women know what I'm talking about. You're out with a guy, it's a pretty nice restaurant, he seems like a decent enough cat, and he goes to the men's room and comes back with this stain on his pants that every female notices. Right? He's thirty, or forty, or fifty, and he's a little successful, and he carries himself okay, and he's walking over to you with this spot on his pants, a blotch the size of a Kennedy half-dollar. It looks like a little Rorschach blot, and it's slowly coming toward you. It's the most incongruous thing. He's had this penis his whole life. You'd think he'd know how to work it by now. How can he not know it's going to spit up and leave a big ol' stain that a woman is going to look at and think, Oh my God, what the hell is that? How could he not know it's there?

Should I mention anything? What do I say? "Excuse me, but you've got urine on your pants. Don't touch anything on this table. Go home and change." But you can't say anything. They see this look on your face and put their hands on your shoulders and ask if everything's okay, and you just want to scream.

I've made a study of this because it makes no sense to me, and I've been with otherwise bright and sensitive guys who were meticulous about their appearance, but the wet spot gets them all, at one time or another. Priests. Teachers. Actors. Hot-shit executives. Presidents. Hey, maybe that's why George Bush threw up when he was over in Japan, a couple years back. He saw the spot on his host's pants after he shook the man's hand, and he just couldn't deal with it.

No one ever says anything, but be advised, gentlemen: We know. We absolutely know.

One of the explanations I've gotten is that when men go to the bathroom they let themselves hang over the porcelain and the urine comes out, and then they think they're done, and then, as they're leaving the bathroom, Mr. Penis says, "I've got a little more." Boom, right into the pants. This happens a lot—enough, you'd think, for a guy to figure out that this little more might be coming. Why not stand and wait for the rest of it? What's the rush? Are you so busy that you can't take the time to go to the bathroom properly? Are you so nervous, standing at the urinal, that some guy's gonna check you out and bust up laughing?

A man will show a woman his penis at the drop of a hat, but he will not show it to another man. Why is that? Some guys worry they're too small, or too narrow, or too funny looking. Some guys worry they'll be hard. Some guys are homophobic. Some guys are self-conscious because they've still got their foreskins. That's a whole other story, honey, the foreskin. The European penises have all got these little hoods on them. You have to work to get to the crux of the European penis. It seems intimidating, the foreskin, like a lot of trouble. I'm told the foreskin makes the penis more sensitive, and I can understand that; if I was covered by a hood all the time, I'd be sensitive too.

It was always a big deal to sneak into the men's room to see what was going on in there, but once you've seen one, you've pretty much seen them all. The mystery's shot. First of all, they've got these strange-looking urinal things built into the floor and wall that look like drooping mouths in a fun-house mirror. They're frightening, really. I hear that in some old ballparks and public buildings they've actually got troughs, around which you guys are supposed to gather for a group pee. I've got no clue what this one's about. I don't get the contemporary urinal either. They step to this porcelain lip, and pull in close so no one sneaks a peek, and if someone steps to the next stall they crunch up tight and hunch forward. There's a real choreography to it.

I've heard that no one stands back a few paces from the urinal and boldly goes about his business. But why not? That's the way they do it when they're out in the woods, or pulled up on the side of the highway. Stick a urinal in someone's bathroom at home, and you'll see guys step back a couple feet before letting fly, but in a public place they're in close for a slam dunk. The problem with this strategy, as I see it, is not only the Kennedy half-dollar of leftover pee, but the rebound pee that flies from the back wall of the urinal and mists the front of your thighs. If you're in too close, and you're wearing a pair of chinos or khakis, you're screwed. You come back looking like you've run through a lawn sprinkler. In jeans, or dark trousers, you can maybe get away with an occasional misting, but you'll be found out by a nose when you get back to your date.

That's another thing I don't get—that guys can't smell it! Why can't they smell it? No one can answer this for me. Doesn't it build up after a while, or start to bake in the sun or ferment at the office? Maybe they do smell it and don't mind. They think, Hell, it's my urine and I'm bringing it back to the table with me. Hell, why not just pee on the table, if that's how it is? Dab some behind your ears and go about your business, because it amounts to the same thing.

So why is it that no one teaches men how to go to the bathroom? This should be a required course of study in any polite society. You'd think that with all the penile pride in this world there would be no issue, that guys would just be shaking their peni until they were bone dry. You'd think there'd be an instruction manual, passed down from father to son, going over some of the finer points of penis maintenance: *You've got to stand there, son, like a big man, and wait for the rest of it to come out. You don't want to go back to the table and greet your date with this little wet spot on your pants that says, "Excuse me, but I didn't have the patience to wait for the rest of it, and it didn't occur to me to dab at it, and I don't give enough of a shit about you to care about this aspect of my appearance."*

Why can't a man dab his penis? No man I know uses toilet paper after he pees. The logic escapes me. I've never seen a men's room with a toilet paper dispenser by the urinal. I don't know why. Men live by the shake, but wiping makes so much more sense. You can't control those last drops of pee when you're just shaking yourself dry. They get on your shoes, or on the next person's shoes, or on the floor in someone's guest bathroom. Who knows where the fuck it goes? There's even a little jingle to justify the phenomenon: *No matter how much you wiggle and dance, the last few drops go down your pants*. Okay, but how about if you wiped? Maybe if you just wiped like the rest of us you wouldn't have this problem.

Most women don't know shit about wiping either, but at least we make the effort. And, man, do we make the effort: We all think we need a bath mitt to wipe. We sit there and we pull and pull and pull, and then we wrap and wrap and wrap, and pull and pull and pull, and we wind up looking like burn victims with these gigantic fists of toilet paper, just to wipe at a couple drops of pee. It's like putting on a suit to make an important phone call. We don't want to get any on our hands because maybe we'll be waving to someone and they'll catch a pee waft and start thinking, you know, What's the deal with her? We go through ten times the amount of toilet paper we need for the job. What's that ad? "A little dab'll do ya." The same goes here. A couple squares of two-ply gets the job done, and we can save a few million acres of our precious trees for some more urgent need.

But women are taught to wipe. We're also taught to change our underwear every day, and maybe even before we go out again at night, in case we get hit by a car and have to go to the hospital. No one should have to see our crusty drawers, but I'm thinking, What's the big deal? Everybody gets crusty drawers, unless we shower after every dump, or walk around with a swab to wipe around the rim. There's always a little residue, no matter how much you wipe. And if you've had one of those Carvel poops, the soft-ice-cream-spiral kind, well, then, you can just forget about coming clean. That shit stays with you.

There are all kinds of ways to wipe. There's the forward wipe, which women know to avoid because it takes the debris from the butt and deposits it in or around the vagina and causes all sorts of problems. Then there's the backhand wipe, but this one is so awkward. You have to go down and backward, and then you have to carry the wet toilet paper and lift your butt and put it in.

We're also taught not to sit down on a public toilet. Never, never, never, no matter what. If you absolutely have to, if there's important, sitting-down business that's not gonna happen any other way, then you wipe the seat down with toilet paper, and make yourself a protective shield out of what's left in the roll. Those prefab, precut sanitary things they've got in some rest rooms are completely useless; they never stay put, and they feel like wax paper. So the only solution—'cause you can't hold it in, which is why you're in the bathroom in the first place—is toilet paper, but even then you've got to sit yourself down carefully so that your toilet paper squares don't slide to the side. I suppose, on a long car trip, you could carry your own bathroom goody bag, with some Handi Wipes, Windex and Lysol, maybe some rubber gloves, your own roll of T.P., and a change of drawers, but few people can plan for such emergencies.

In a pinch, you try to straddle the bowl and leave your butt up in the air and point your stream down in the water and hope that the angle doesn't leave you peeing on your shoes, or right into your pants. Yes, this happens sometimes. You never know which way it's gonna go. We're pretty good shots, but there's so much running through our fussy little heads—germs, the green spot on the seat, the smell (oh, that smell!)—that we sometimes miss our target. Little girls have a particular problem with this because they can't lift their butts over the bowl with their feet still on the ground. You could try one of those Mary Lou Retton pommel-horse moves, but you'd have to brace each leg up the walls on either side of the can, or brace against the seat, and who the hell wants to brace against the seat and touch it with their bare hands? Anyway, this requires the kind of strength and agility most little girls don't have unless they've been training with Bela Karolyi since the age of four.

Sometimes, with toddlers, you see these mothers cradling their little girls over the public toilet like they were Elmo dolls, and the kid's butt may be spared all those unknown germs, but there's still no guarantee that the stream is not gonna just run down the mother's arm.

You'd think we'd have this business figured out, but people have huge problems with it, you know. It comes up in conversation, this wet spot phenomenon, and guys just don't get that their not wiping has me all freaked out. They don't see that an extra drop or two on the tip of their penis is any kind of problem. "It's just me," they'll say, as if this makes it okay. "It's just pee." Or here's my favorite:

"What's the big deal? You've had it in your mouth." Do you mean to tell me that before you put it in my mouth, you didn't wash it off? Is this what you're telling me? You didn't wipe? Even beasts lick themselves clean. They don't ask the queen of the jungle to do it for them. What kind of pompous fuck doesn't take the time to wash off his dick before sticking it in the mouth of the person he loves?

There's a tremendous arrogance, I think, in the way men disregard their difficulties with urine maintenance, and it flows from this whole penis thing they've got going on in their heads. Sometimes it seems it's all they talk about. They build monuments to it, write songs about it, use it to beat back Darth Vader. If everything else went away and the penis was still alive, men would probably be okay with that. They'd be lying there thinking, Well, at least my dick still works.

But, gentlemen, your precious little fellas are not above the laws of polite society. He needs to be washed. You need to clean up after him. Let's work together on this one. Let's leave some toilet paper by the urinals in the men's room. We women will use a little less, so you can have the extra. Let's make the effort. Let's try to remember that if you don't wipe, you're gonna walk around with this pissy smell that everyone else in the room can pick up on except you. That wet spot may fade, but the memory will not.

And while we're on it, check this out: You're not as big as you think, and not as small as you fear, and most women don't really give a shit either way. Grab yourself all you want, but grab on to the fact that the world doesn't end at the tip of your penis.

TALK

HERE'S MY THEORY: Sally, Geraldo, Jenny, Montel, Jerry . . . all those people are just doing *Queen for a Day,* without the prize. No, really. In the old days, on *Queen for a Day* or *Truth or Consequences,* at least you could root for the people to take home a prize, or reunite with a long-lost loved one, or reclaim a little hope or dignity, but now we're rooting against them.

We've done a complete turn. We seem to have lost the ability to see these poor people win by losing. We judge without compassion, and believe we have the answers to their lives. It's therapy without understanding. We sit at home, or in the studio audience, and we're full of You didn'ts . . . You ought tos . . . You should'ves. The mike passes to the next indignant participant, and we have to ask ourselves, are these people any better for the exercise? Let's ask Jenny . . .

You couldn't really do *Queen for a Day* now, it wouldn't fly. But these afternoon talk shows play to the same parts of our heads. It's the same drill. You come on the show, and you tell the most horrible, most unbelievable story, and somebody gives you a prize for having the worst luck. Remember? "My husband hit me with the car, he ran me over, then I crawled fifty-two blocks to the hospital where I fell in a manhole, and then as I climbed out of the manhole a brick fell from one of the hospital windows and gashed me in the face." Music cue. "Johnny, what do we have for her today?" And you're sitting at home thinking, Yes, give her the washing machine, give her the console television, give her whatever she wants.

I'd watch and think, That's a tough life, you know. Yeah, good for you. You need that new dishwasher, or console television. You go, girl. We all passed judgment, and weighed whose life was worse, ours or theirs, and we got to see their life get better, if only for a minute. And no matter how great those prizes were, all of us at home were happy it wasn't us up there on the screen.

The guests on today's daytime shows are still getting screwed, which is why they're invited on, but now they do a quarter turn and get screwed for the cameras. They should at least hold out for a prize, for something they need or really want. Every week, at the end of the week, Sally Jessy should give away a car, or an appliance, or a Windsurfer. You know, just pluck the most pathetic creatures from her ranks and put little crowns on their heads and play some weepy music and give away some stuff. And then maybe at the end of the season they can trade it all in for even bigger prizes. Make it like a game show. You there, the transvestite, do you want to go up against the battered woman and play for a chance at a Caribbean cruise? Or do you want to go up against the gothically obsessed six-year-old from Oklahoma? Who will take the prize?

I'm tellin' you, the suspense would beat all.

I think it helps to look at these lurid talk shows as the love child of those old game shows. It sets it all in perspective. Put the cells of *Queen for a Day* and *Let's Make a Deal* in a petri dish, refrigerate ("in a brand-new Amana!"), and in a couple years you wind up with Jenny Jones. It's a natural progression, when you break it down. On *Let's Make a Deal,* Monty Hall would just walk up and down those old bleachers he had set up and pluck out the most outrageous characters he could find, whoever he thought would be uninhibited or fun or a little out there. It's the same impulse, and then he'd dangle the bait of cash money and prizes and vacations in front of these folks and get them to make asses of themselves on national television.

I used to think about what I'd wear on Monty's show. You didn't see many black faces in that crowd, so I figured I'd have to come up with something creative, just to get in the door. I might have gone as a black-eyed Susan, with big yellow things around my face. Play to my strength. A freckle would have worked, and it wouldn't have been much of a stretch in terms of costuming, but I'm not sure old Monty would have understood it. That's the thing: You had to get Monty to dig what you were about, or he'd just pass you by. A coffee bean would have been good. That wouldn't have threatened anyone, and maybe the Maxwell House people would have hired me as a spokesperson. I could have taken an eyebrow pencil and drawn lines down my face and gone as a raisin. You couldn't be too subtle with Monty, though. You had to grab his attention and wrestle it to the ground.

Match Game, Hollywood Squares, Password . . . I loved all those shows. I'd root for the people and listen to all the celebrity small talk and think it was all so glamorous. To go on *Password* and give clues to Professor Irwin Corey was to rub up against greatness. I didn't know, as a kid, that a lot of people thought the celebrities they snagged for these shows were kinda on the downsides of their careers. All I knew was they were on television, so they were famous. And funny. Charles Nelson Reilly. Brett Somers. Paul Lynde. JoAnne Worley. Charlie Weaver. The crew.

Dick Clark's *$20,000 Pyramid,* now that was a show. That was hard. It looked like a breeze, but the category was never something obvious, like "Things People Say to Someone on Their Birthday," because, you know, then it would've just been "Happy Birthday," or, "How old are you now?" They tried to trip you up. "Things Nelson Rockefeller Would Buy at a Yard Sale." "Things Adulterers Say to Each Other in Bars." Something you had to think about, but you only had sixty seconds to think about it, and you had to think how the celebrity was thinking and where he was coming from. The regular people would just freeze up, playing that game; they'd get all crinkly and serious, like they were working toward world peace. The celebrities would freeze up, too, only they knew how to make a joke out of it; they let the tension roll from them, and then they fell all over themselves apologizing when they cost the regular contestant a chance at the big money. That was always the real drama, when the gal from Gainesville could've taken home $25,000 if Norman Fell had known the difference between an eggplant and a squash. I loved when it hinged on small shit like that. I loved the way the celebrities put on their eyeglasses, to show they were really concentrating, and the way Dick Clark would lean over and get all earnest and ask, "Do you want to give, or do you want to receive?" You couldn't ask that question today in most settings, and yet he made it sound like it was the most important decision these people would ever have to make—and for many of them, I suppose it was.

These shows are mostly gone now, except for *Jeopardy!* and *Wheel of Fortune*. *Wheel of Fortune* I can't deal with. I don't understand the point. My mind doesn't work that way. *Jeopardy!* I like. I play the shit out of it at home, but *Celebrity Jeopardy*? No can do. I'd freeze up like Ralph Kramden when he had his shot at a game show. I'd be all flustered and stammering and pretending my buzzer didn't work. That's the only way to save face on *Jeopardy!*—pretend your buzzer doesn't work. Shake that thing like you're really trying to lock in and give the answer. Don't waste your time the night before boning up on "Cities in Nepal," or "Pets of the Bible." Take an acting class. Stand in front of the mirror and work on looking exasperated. It's the only way to keep from embarrassing yourself.

The Price Is Right is another one that's still around, and this will never cease to shock the shit out of me. Here's a show where the greatest accomplishment is to be a good shopper; if you comparison-shop and clip coupons, you're all set. They call your name, you guess the price, you try to choke the host. What's that about? It's greed.

It's the American Dream. It's a soap opera disguised as a game show. The *Price Is Right* people break into tears when they win the showcase round. The contestants fall to their knees and thank their maker, because they get to take home a new dining-room set, or a reclining chair, or a fucking motor boat. The producers of these shows don't tell these people they'll owe like a shitload of money in taxes, calculated on the full retail value of their prizes, because that would kinda spoil the moment, you know. They save that part for later.

There's no place on television anymore for the strange mix of real people and celebrities, the way they had on those game shows from the sixties and seventies. It was an important part of the equation. A housewife from Nebraska could actually sit down and play a game *with* Hope Lange or the guy who played the manager on *The Partridge Family*. It was kinda like having them over for a hand of bridge. There was a real nobleman-commoner sensibility to the whole setup, and that's missing from our popular culture today. Daytime television is all about sleeping with your mother's boyfriend, or telling your kid that if she's got trouble breathing on account of her deviated septum then she probably shouldn't have pierced her nose. The nighttime talk shows, Letterman and Leno, have become pretty predictable. There's a scripted anecdote or two, and a plug for a new movie or album or book, but there's no real conversational humor. Even a show like *Politically Incorrect,* which probably gets closer to intellectual spontaneity than any other current talk show, is really just about four famous people trying to get the floor to show how smart they are.

• • •

I had my own turn, a couple years back. I did a late-night talk show that I thought could kinda counter everything else that was on at the time. Not too many people watched, at least not in television terms, but then television is probably the only place where one million people can enjoy what you do and you still turn up a failure.

I don't set this out to blow smoke up my own ass, because ultimately my show didn't succeed, but for me the effort was all about hearing people talk. I didn't have a band, or a sidekick, or a monologue. My guests weren't out on the talk-show circuit, plugging some new project. I didn't ask them who they were fucking, 'cause I could read that shit in the *Enquirer* and, frankly, I didn't care. I didn't get folks to tell me that same anecdote they'd been tellin' on all the other talk shows, 'cause I could hear that on all the other talk shows. I just wanted 'em to relax, and be themselves, and say what was on their minds. Talk. That's why these things were called talk shows in the first place.

So that was the goal, and I invited all kinds of interesting people to come on the show and talk about interesting things. I wanted to know what other people thought about all kinds of shit, and figured if I provided an environment where it wasn't about somebody's scandal, or somebody's movie, then we could just take a look at what was going on.

I had some great people on my show. A real eclectic bunch. Alexander Haig came on. I asked him how he'd like to be addressed. General Haig? Mr. Haig? He just said, "Call me Big Al." I thought, Cool. Big Al's on the show.

Tom Metzger came on, and I took a lot of heat 'cause I just let him hang himself. I didn't tighten the noose. I just let him talk. I thought, Okay, I want to hear what this man is about, and if I challenge him he ain't gonna come clean. So I listened. I got ripped for not presenting other people's opinions, for not ripping into him with mine, but I wanted the audience at home to think how *they* felt. Not how I felt. Not how other people felt. How *they* felt. I tried to stay neutral, and this man was expecting the same old shit. He was expecting me to challenge him. He'd say something like, "Black people should go back where they came from," and I'd just say, "Really?" You know, very neutral. "This should be a country for white people," he'd say. "You have Africa." And then I'd say, "No, actually I don't. I think I predate you. My people have been here longer than yours." And then I cut to commercial.

He's an interesting cat, that Tom Metzger. He asked for my autograph when we were in a break. Said he was a huge fan. His kids are fans. But there's one of him on every side of every issue. They see things their own way. After he was on, I got a call from the head of the Jewish Anti-Defamation League, and he said he wanted to come on to challenge some of Metzger's positions, and I did the same thing with him. He couldn't believe I gave Metzger that kind of rope, but he was just as bad. He had no clue. He kept talking about *our* neighborhoods and *their* neighborhoods, and I kept saying, "Whose neighborhood are you talking about? Just who are *they*?" He tried to dance his way out of it, said it didn't matter, said it was the people who don't keep their neighborhoods as clean as we keep ours. You know. He was just another facet of Tom Metzger. He thought he was the rebuttal, but he was just more of the same, and if I'd yelled and screamed and done all that stuff, no one would have realized that. But if you just shut up and let people talk, they hang themselves. They hang themselves.

For me, the show was about listening. And making my guests comfortable. I always asked them, at the end of the show, if there was anything we talked about that they wanted to cut from the interview. I thought, you know, this wasn't a news show. I wasn't a journalist. I wasn't out to make people look bad, or have them regret coming on. I wanted them to come back. I understood that it was a vulnerable situation, with no studio audience and all; you kinda forgot the cameras were there. But no one ever asked me to cut anything out. If there was something sensitive, or surprising, they said we should keep it in. They said they must have needed to say it, or it wouldn't have come out of their mouths in the first place.

Al Gore came on during the 1992 campaign, and he was talking about his position on this and that, and somehow it led to his kids. He told about watching his son get hit by a car and dragged down the street. He did this complete shift from politician to parent in, like, no time. It was extraordinary. Suddenly, there was this person in front of me. He wasn't this stiff politician, but a human being, talking about a real human moment.

I flashed on my own kid. I just got this image of my own kid getting hit by a car and I thought, Oh, shit. I asked Senator Gore what he felt, standing there when something like that happens to your kid. He said he felt powerless, to have to just stand there, watching this happen, willing his body to run. It was a complete transformation from the way he'd let himself be known, and from that point on in the interview he couldn't get back to the politician. He continued on as the man.

When we were through I asked him if he was okay with what he'd just said, and he had to think about it for a bit, but finally he said he thought it was fine. And it was. It wasn't a planned disclosure, but once he put it out there he was okay with it.

Hosting that show was like hosting a great dinner party, only your guests came one at a time and other people got to watch you eat. Man, it was a blast. I sang with the Temps, and hung out with Elizabeth Taylor and Tony Bennett and all kinds of cool people. Wayne Newton came on when he was going through some personal-bankruptcy shit, and he was getting pretty beat up over it in the tabloids, and I didn't want to go near the money issue. It was so totally not what the show was about. But the segment producer kept saying, "No, no, he's cool with it, he's got a sense of humor about it, we should do something." She wore me down. Finally, we set up this bit with a checkbook and everything and she kept insisting he'd be fine with it. I should trust her, she said.

So Wayne Newton came on the show, and I handed him this checkbook, and we'd put a little calculator in there, and I told him maybe it would help him to balance his account or something. This was the part where he was supposed to have a sense of humor about the ordeal, right? Well, he took the book, looked over at me, and said, "Fuck you." Just like that: "Fuck you." Then he stood up and walked off the set.

I thought, Shit, you know. This wasn't what I wanted to do. This wasn't how it was supposed to play. Shit. I was completely stunned, and shaken. Wayne was a friend. I wanted to kick myself for not talking to him first, but this producer kept insisting it would be funnier if it was unrehearsed, if we just surprised him with it. Yeah, right.

Then I heard all this laughing backstage. It was Wayne's laugh. There's no mistaking Wayne's laugh. I thought, What the hell is going on? They set me up. Wayne set me up. He wanted me to know that it didn't matter to him. We all go through all kinds of things in life. Bankruptcy was just his thing, at that moment. He wasn't ashamed of it, and he wasn't above having some fun with it, but he knew I'd never bring it up on my own, so he had the producer work a little number on me. And it was funny. He got me good, and it was funny.

But there seems to be no place for this kind of talk on television. Charlie Rose gives great talk, but I don't think he could do what he does on network television. People don't want to listen to G. Gordon Liddy get all weird and scary about Nixon and the future of this country. It's dark, and the people want light. They want *The Tonight Show*, and why not? It's part of our culture. It's comedy. It's a nice diversion. People have a right to their celebrity pap. I got off on it as a kid, so what the hell.

But these afternoon talk shows trouble me. They're not about the guests anymore. They're about us. They're about how we respond to whatever freak show they're putting on. The format begs this kind of mob mentality from the studio audience. The people rip these guests apart. They scream, "Yeah, yeah, you're a bitch," and then they cut to commercial and pretend there's some sort of resolution, but there's never any real resolution. The fucked-up people on the panel are gonna leave the show as fucked up as they were when they arrived. Shit, they're probably even more fucked up by the way these people have stood in judgment over their lives and the choices they've made. The audience is like a lynch mob, and some of these guests probably feel lucky to get out of the studio alive, but then when they get back to their hometowns, the lynch mobs are probably camping by their front doors. Really, how do people show their faces after the kinds of shit they reveal on national television?

It tells me we're not all that far from televising our executions. It's the next step. First we uplift these people and make their lives better by giving them a prize and a little attention, then we degrade them, then we judge them, then we pull up a chair and fire up a bowl of popcorn and check out their execution. Who the fuck's gonna sponsor that? Next, on *Jenny's Public Execution,* John "I-Eat-Human-Beings" Smith. Applause, applause, applause. Today's method? Firing squad. Applause, applause, applause. Brought to you by Mr. Clean, the heavy-duty cleaner. We'll clean up this bloody mess after we kill this bastard. G.E. could sponsor the electric chair, and maybe some pharmaceutical company could handle the lethal injections.

Is this where we're headed? Are these shows just little bricks in the road that's gonna take us there? Can we do something about it? I'm not sure. Maybe if we start talking to each other instead of at each other. Maybe if we do like Lucy in *Peanuts* and set up little booths and let our friends and neighbors air their shit on a more personal level. Maybe if we get people to understand that airing their shit on national television does not mean resolution. It just means a whole lot more people will know about your shit. Maybe if we pool our money and start outbidding these talk show producers for their guests. What's that? Sally Jessy's gonna pay you four hundred dollars to come on her air and talk about how your daddy raped the prize cow and now you're a cross-dresser? Well, how 'bout if I pay you five hundred dollars *not* to talk about it? Stay home. Talk to your friends. Talk to your daddy, if he's still around. Or better still, talk to a shrink. Yeah, I understand you need to get something off your chest, but just take the five hundred dollars and keep it to yourself. Scratch the surface and realize that we all got shit to deal with; we just don't need to deal with it on a public stage. Sally and Jenny can't figure this stuff out for you. The answer to your problems is not on television. Don't let these people judge you, because then you'll just be like them, and pretty soon we'll all just be like them, and then we're all screwed, honey. Then we're done.

TASTE

THE IDEA OF eliminating the National Endowment for the Arts in this country sends a chill down my spine and a bug up my butt. As I write this, there's a proposal kicking around to cut the NEA budget from an already-slashed $99 million all the way down to $10 million, which would basically be enough to shut the agency down, and I just don't get it. First of all, I don't get why it costs $10 million just to shut the endowment down. If you've got to close your doors, then close your doors, but if you've got a final $10 million to work with, why not spread it around? It may not go very far, but it'll go.

Mostly what I don't get is why the Republican Congress wants to shut down the agency at all. Okay, so there've been some artists in recent years who've received government grants whose work was not for everybody. Robert Mapplethorpe was not for everybody. But does that mean his art should be discounted? Should all controversial artists be cut off? Should museums that exhibit controversial works be cut off? And just because one man's art is controversial and out there, should our more mainstream artists be cut off as well? What does Robert Mapplethorpe have to do with the ballet, or the symphony, or the children's art programs in your community?

There's a quote in *The New York Times* from an Ohio congressman named Bob Ney, a Republican, who apparently doesn't have time to read a book, or take in a play, or listen to opera. Or maybe he's got the time, but there's no percentage in it. It's not a good career move, this art thing. "It is time to get the federal government out of the business of subsidizing art," this man said. "I support the arts and humanities. However, I believe that during an era of fiscal belt tightening, funding of the NEA by the federal government should not be a top priority."

Yeah, right. I support the air we breathe, but there's no money in the budget to pay for it. Without the NEA, all the opera companies and theater companies and artists' groups that go into schools to teach all kinds of shit, they're all gone. All the people who write about subjects that major publishers are not interested in publishing, gone. All those small community presses that had been getting some funding from the NEA, gone. Painters, sculptors, photographers, performance artists, gone.

Okay, here's a little homework assignment. Go to your local library and find out how much NEA monies have been kicking around in your community—for your local theater, or your local old people's pottery programs, or even for the library itself—and measure what you like against what you don't like. Consider all those positive programs alongside all of the offensive programs in receipt of agency grants. I bet the ratio of safe, acceptable art to offensive art is about the same as the ratio of safe, acceptable congressmen and senators to offensive congressmen and senators, and yet you don't hear anyone suggesting we should throw out the House and the Senate. Well, Mr. Gingrich, I don't like what you're doing down there in Washington, so I think we'll just abolish this little democratic government we've got going and let the people figure it out for themselves.

For my money, art is about shaking people up and making them look at their world in new ways. If literature and cinema and dance and theater didn't clash with our public morals from time to time, we'd be without such treasures as *The Grapes of Wrath,* or *Midnight Cowboy,* or any of Alvin Ailey's suggestive dance pieces, or even the tits and ass of a great musical like *A Chorus Line*. We'd be without Robert Mapplethorpe, and whatever your take on Mapplethorpe, there's no denying that the cat makes you scratch your head a little bit and try on a different view. If you're offended, stay away, but don't cut the rest of us off. If Andres Serrano's cross lying in a pool of urine is just not your thing, then it's just not your thing, so stay home. Last time I looked, there was not that much urine in the museums, but maybe I missed something.

So check it out. How much money did your community get, and where did it go? How many school programs did it fund? How many old-people programs did it fund? Add all that up, and look at the programs you found somewhat objectionable, and weigh those against all the assholes in the Senate and the House in the next column, and things'll probably even out. This exercise won't do us any good, because the NEA will just be gone, but it'll be good to know as we head back into the Dark Ages.

Art is long, life is short. Unless your funding is fucked, in which case all our days are numbered.

DREAM

I CAN DO ANYTHING. I can be anything. No one ever told me I couldn't. No one ever expressed this idea that I was limited to any one thing, and so I think in terms of what's possible, not impossible.

They did sell me on the notion of reality. That I got. I got the laws of physics and nature pretty much down and knew early on there were very specific things I couldn't do. I knew I could never make anyone float, or turn water into wine, or make cats speak French. I knew I couldn't bring people back from the dead. I got that part of it. But I also knew that if I was with someone who had lost somebody I might be able to make them feel better. I couldn't keep someone's house from burning down, but I could help them sort through the rubble and get their shit together and start in on another one. So I realized I wasn't God, which was a slight disappointment, you know. Just a slight disappointment—and a mild surprise.

Movies were my first window to the outside world, and they told me stuff. They told me I could go anywhere, be whatever I wanted, solve any damn puzzle. The right movie was my ticket to any place I wanted to go. But it had to be the right movie, and it had to come from the right place, 'cause I had to bank on it being historically accurate. See, in school, nobody talked about black people unless they had us picking cotton. Who knew there were free blacks? Maybe you heard about Frederick Douglass, but you didn't really know about Frederick Douglass. You couldn't always trust the history books. They told a diluted truth, a truth by committee. It was only later that I learned there was something missing in what went down with the landed Americans and the indigenous people of this country. In movies too. They didn't always get the story right, especially when it came to our nonwhite history. You knew the Indians didn't look like Jeffrey Hunter, but you didn't know what they really looked like either. It was a great mystery. There weren't too many Indians in my Catholic school in New York, so you had to use your imagination a little bit.

In my head, Queen Elizabeth was just like Bette Davis. That's how I saw her. She walked and talked and *poof*ed—and made grand statements in staccato sentences. Movies opened doors to a lot of things for me, but for every one they opened another one closed. The casting always messed with the way I saw it. It changed the terms. In this way, books were more liberating, more magical, and so I started to read. To really *read*. Books opened the mind to all kinds of possibilities. There is nothing in Dickens to leave you thinking there were no black people in England, or that Bob Cratchit didn't pass you on the street every single day. But movies made you believe there were no black people, except the ones who were picking cotton, or tap-dancing up a flight of stairs, or birthin' babies. When I was little, this didn't strike me as odd, but as I grew up, all during the 1960s, it bothered the shit out of me. I knew there had to be more to us than that. Now I know there are all-black movies, with gumshoes and heroes, cowboys and harlots, but these were just not shown on the *Million Dollar Movie,* and when I started to figure this out I realized life was what we put in and took out, and we were all in the same soup. Indians, blacks, Asians, women . . . Shit, it never even occurred to me that Emma *wasn't* black. It wasn't a part of the equation. Why shouldn't we have been in a Jane Austen situation? Why wouldn't we have been in a manor house in a Dickens novel? Why couldn't we have been the light in the forest? And don't tell me Robert Louis Stevenson didn't have me in mind when he wrote *Treasure Island,* because, you know, even the Muppets understand this notion.

Daydreaming, I used to think I was Sherlock Holmes; it's a part I've always wanted to play. If you're the most brilliant detective, the people will come to you. They won't care if you're black, or a woman. It might even give the story some new dimensions. *The Speckled Band,* starring Whoopi Goldberg. I like it!

This—the possibility—is why I look on acting as such a joyous thing. It's shot through with possibility. Anything can happen. As I write this, I'm appearing eight times a week, on Broadway, in a part originally written for a man, but you'd never know, right? If you come to a thing with no preconceived notions of what that thing is, the whole world can be your canvas. Just dream it, and you can make it so. I believe I belong wherever I want to be, in whatever situation or context I place myself. I believed I could pass as an ancient Roman in *A Funny Thing Happened on the Way to the Forum*. I believed a little girl could rise from a single-parent household in the Manhattan projects, start a single-parent household of her own, struggle through seven years of welfare and odd jobs, and still wind up making movies. You can go from anonymity to Planet Hollywood and never lose sight of where you've been.

So, yeah, I think anything is possible. I know it because I have lived it. I know it because I have seen it. I have witnessed things the ancients would have called miracles, but they are not miracles. They are the products of someone's dream, and they happen as the result of hard work. Or they happen because, you know, shit happens. As human beings, we are capable of creating a paradise, and making each other's lives better by our own hands. Yes, yes, yes . . . this is possible.

If something hasn't happened, it's not because it can't happen, or won't; it just hasn't happened yet. If I haven't done something, I just haven't gotten around to it. For a long time, I wanted to sit with Stephen Hawking and have him explain all his theories to me so that I could understand them and build on them and find ways to adapt them to my own life. But I never got around to that. I would like to be a diplomat in some foreign country for a couple months. I would like to play for the Knicks, and dance with Alvin Ailey, and ride a camel down Sunset Boulevard. I would like to find a way to stop famine, and to free the children from the orphanages in Bosnia, Rwanda, and Romania, and here at home. I would like to do a lot of things. All I need is time.

HELP

I'VE GOT TWO TRAINS running on this one, so stay with me and we'll take 'em to the same station.

One of the things I've been thinking about during the months spent writing this book is this inability a lot of us have to ask for help. Why is that? I see it in myself. As you'll know if you've read this far in the book, I think I can do everything. If I don't do it myself, it won't be done right, you know. So I never pull up and say, "Listen, I don't know what the fuck I'm doing." I never ask for help, at least not at first. It's not in my nature.

What brought this to mind was what's been happening to our affirmative action programs around the country, over the past while, and what happened to me during the writing of this book. I'll deal with the larger issue first. There's a lot wrong with the move to kill affirmative action in this country, because we do not yet live in a world with equal opportunities for all people. We just don't. Blacks. Hispanics. Women. Veterans. The disabled. There are all kinds of folks who are just not on any kind of level playing field, and yet I open the paper every day and read of some state tearing down some program as if the need for affirmative action had miraculously disappeared. I read all this shit, and I start to wonder, If we dismantle affirmative action, how will people pull up and ask for help? Where's that reflex gonna come from? And how are people gonna act on it? Without affirmative action, if you are in fact disadvantaged, there'll be no place for you. Yeah, quotas aren't necessarily the answer, but for a lot of people quotas are the best shot, and if you take that shot away those people are left at the door.

So there had been that train, running through my head, and alongside it I had this book. Now, I'm no Henry James. I know that. I'm no Calvin Trillin. Never said I was. And yet there I was, struggling to put my thoughts on paper, and even though it wasn't going like I wanted it to be going, I just couldn't pull up and ask for help.

Dan Paisner, my spook, was not a welcome addition to this project initially, at least not by me. See, I went about writing this book in a very unusual way. Most people put pen to paper, but I've never been that kind of writer. I have to work my shit out on my feet, and then, after I've done it, I can finally set it down. But that's not how you write a book. I tried. I know. So I got a court reporter, who came and sat with me and a couple other people, and I talked, and out of those sessions I produced these two wonderful transcripts, with all of my spacey pauses, and non sequiturs, and all the things that happen when I begin to talk and I have to take these moments to connect things, because even I don't know what the fuck I'm saying. I sat for the longest time with these two not-quite books, trying to figure out what to make of them, and I kept reading them thinking that I was just pants-down in front of the audience. The transcripts didn't at all represent what I wanted this book to be.

Finally, it was suggested I find someone to help me organize all this material. The stuff was there, the point was made; I just needed someone to help me get to it. And I thought, Hell, no. *I'm* writing this book. *I'm* putting this down. I don't want anybody's help. Because, of course, I think I'm God. (We've covered that, right?) But then, after some real thought, I said, "Well, maybe there's something to this." I was doing *Forum* on Broadway, I was in the middle of my run, and I had the rest of my life going, and it wasn't like I was up in Nantucket, you know, in a little house, writing. Suddenly the idea of having someone come and help me organize what was in my head and in these transcripts seemed not such a bad idea after all.

So in came Dan, who listened and said, "Well, is that what you really mean?" Or, "Okay, that's a good point, but if you follow this line here it'll take you to a better one." He told me it's one thing if you *say* it, but it's another thing if you *write* it. You have to have some sort of structure. You have to know where you're going. And you have to realize that if you say this, that, and some other thing, it begs a whole other string of questions. You can't go there, without also going here. You've got to think it through, you know. So not only was I receiving some help in structuring the material, but I was revisiting it, and enlarging it, and creating new material. Mostly, though, what I was doing was learning, and there's nothing wrong with learning.

Shortly after Dan and I had gotten together, an article appeared in *The New York Times Magazine,* talking about ghostwriters and celebrities who didn't have the time or the experience or the patience to write their books themselves. The author's take seemed to be that there was something wrong with having to rely on a ghostwriter to do the job, and that people like myself, who are writers of their own material in some other medium, should be above asking for help to translate what they do into book form. The article offended me more and more each time I thought about it, and what pissed me off was the way the writer—who had never written a book, to my knowledge, because they've got that little thing under the article that says what he's done and it didn't say nothing 'bout no book—seemed to say there was no place for my kind of book, because I'm *not* Calvin Trillin, because I couldn't do it myself.

Well, so the fuck what? The writer even pointed his finger directly at me. He reported that Whoopi Goldberg had "landed" a contract to write her "pensées" and "then boasted that she would not use a ghost." Now, I didn't "land" any such thing, and I never set out to write my "pensées," and I certainly didn't "boast" about doing it myself. I meant to try, that's all, and when it turned out I couldn't quite pull it off because I was limited by what I knew, I looked for help.

Still, the reporter went on to doubt that my editor would let this book pass only through my typewriter. "When it appears," he cautioned, "check the acknowledgments carefully." So these words are my acknowledgments. Read them carefully. Yes, I had help writing this book, and yes, I thank Dan Paisner from the bottom of my heart. And to the guy who wrote the *Times* article, fuck off. Until you've walked a mile in my shoes, you can't know how deep the snow really is.

All of which takes me in a roundabout way back to affirmative action. Throughout the writing of this book, I read about the California schools and started to look on Dan, my spook, as my own little affirmative-action program. After all, affirmative action was meant to take people to where they could say, "Hey, I can't do this on my own." For whatever reason. Maybe it's because we live in a country built on the notion of property, and some of us were once considered property, and we've never quite been able to get that off the books or out of our heads. Who knows?

The idea, whether it be in something as banal as needing help to write a book, or as important as your kid being able to go to the school of her choice, is the same. If she does the work, your kid should be able to go to The Citadel and not have to deal with a whole lot of bullshit. She'll deal with the bullshit when she's in there, 'cause that's a whole other deal, but she should have the opportunity to prove herself. It's important.

I don't know how this happened, or when, but we've stopped thinking it's okay to ask for help. We still ask, some of us, and we still receive, but there's a taint to it that doesn't need to be there. Welfare is help. Ghostwriters are help. Affirmative action is help. Head Start and child care are help. A.A. is help. (Even A.A.A. is help.) Shit, we all need help from each other—in one way or another, at one time or another—and yet there's something awful happening out there, where people think asking for help is not a good thing. We're far enough from the heat to discover that we've become cold. Those pictures of black people getting knocked down by fire hoses, dogs biting their legs, those images are far enough away to let people say it's all fine now. But it ain't. It ain't.

So I figure in about twenty-five years we'll have affirmative action back on the ballots, and maybe I will have learned how to write by then, like a formal essayist, but I don't know if that will be a good thing. I might really prefer to have someone take the craziness out of my head and organize it in a way that people can follow, because I really do believe I'm some sort of alien.

But that's for the next book.